The Wild Places of Britain

The Wild Places of Britain

David Bellamy

Foreword by John Hillaby

Webb & Bower

MICHAEL JOSEPH

To Mum, who still tells me not to go into those
awful mountains if it's raining

First published in Great Britain 1986 by
Webb & Bower (Publishers) Limited
9 Colleton Crescent, Exeter, Devon EX2 4BY

in association with Michael Joseph Limited
27 Wright's Lane, London W8 5SL

Designed by Peter Wrigley

Production by Nick Facer

British Library Cataloguing in Publication Data

Bellamy, David, 1933–
    The wild places of Britain.
    1. Great Britain – Description and travel – 1971 – Views
    I. Title
    914.1'04858'0222   DA632

ISBN 0–86350–116–8

Typeset in Great Britain by
Keyspools Ltd., Golborne, Lancashire.

Printed and bound in Hong Kong by
Mandarin Offset International Ltd.

TITLE PAGE: Rannoch Moor in Winter

CONTENTS

St Oswald's Church, Horton in Ribblesdale

After dinner I walked the short distance to the church in borrowed boots two sizes too small: my own were falling to bits. Sheltering from the rain in a doorway, I painted the church with Pen-y-Ghent rising in the background, standing on one leg at a time to ease the pain of the pinching boots. Hardly had I begun the composition when a sheepdog appeared, took a liking to me, and wrapped both front paws round my leg. We almost toppled over as I tried to break free. I hopped to a better position, but the dog followed, still firmly anchored. Eventually I retired, hopping, to my lodgings.

FOREWORD

When Corot used to go out painting early on misty summer mornings he always knocked off work within an hour of sunrise saying, 'Everything can be seen now, and so there's nothing more to see'. For him the half amounted to far more than the whole. As soon as the very elements of a landscape emerged from thoughtful obscurity, he wanted no more of it. And as you turn over the pages that follow, pages which for me, a fairly well-travelled Yorkshireman, are more remedial than any medicine I know of, I hope you will agree that David Bellamy is a master at image-making. It is just that – and I must point out that I didn't say 'simply that' – he has the extra-normal gift of the poet's eye. At all times, especially during storms, places speak to him and no matter whether he knows or doesn't know the mineralogical difference between, say, Carboniferous Limestone and its geological bedfellows, the grits or the much younger dolerite which is lava, he can interpret, visually, the landscapes they have made, landscapes as distinctive as fingerprints or lines of braille or facial differences between this race and that.

Look at Pen-y-Ghent behind Horton church. I have seen that crouching lion a dozen times from the top of Fountains Fell. Some mountains are much given to whispering. Pen-y-Ghent never does. It's always listening. You may ignore the sexual content of Gaping Gill but never the thought that it's the sort of place where Orpheus might well have gone down to hell to look for Eurydice. Goredale Scar, like Cheddar Gorge, is obviously a cave from the long bygone days of dinosaurs, the roof of which has fallen in. These were the scenes of my boyhood.

It has never occurred to me that a man is more or less of a villain because he happens to have been born within sight of the moors or the mountains or lives above the Thames Estuary as I do now, mostly. But for a painter or a writer to be able to return to the scenes of childhood, as salmon do after much wandering, is a privilege. And in looking over this selection I feel hugely in debt to David Bellamy, who has such a sure sense of place.

JOHN HILLABY

Ramshaw Rocks, North Staffordshire

I
SKETCHING IN THE WILDS

Sunlight sparkled on the ice-axe as it flashed through the air and embedded itself in wet snow. Overhead towered great sandstone buttresses, whilst below me the southern aspect of Liathach fell away sharply over 2500 feet. So far the climb had progressed well and the sunshine lured me into a languid complacency. Suddenly my foot slipped and I fell, dangling over the void from the ice-axe. Frantically I grasped at a rock with my left hand, and to my relief felt its solid assurance. I clung on for dear life. It had happened too quickly for it to be frightening, but my heart pounded as I snatched a glance downwards. Automatically my toecaps kicked into the snow, which promptly fell away from my exposed position. Hauling myself up over an ice-covered rock, I inwardly cursed my laziness in not fastening on crampons earlier. The snow was atrociously unmanageable and collapsed at the slightest provocation. I recovered my breath and resumed climbing. My gaze kept returning to the buttresses of Coire Leith, until I could resist it no longer. The scene begged to be sketched; but how? A short climb, then I roped onto a suitable rock and began sketching. The rope was a constant reminder of my lofty perch, and, if I did happen to inadvertently step back to check the painting, its presence would prevent a total disaster.

Since the latter part of the eighteenth century mountains have been popular subjects with artists. Before that the wild places were regarded with considerable awe as can be seen from the diaries of early travellers. People had been too afraid of the 'horrors' of the mountains to venture onto them for pleasure. At the end of the eighteenth century it was almost felt obligatory for an artist to visit the Lake District or North

Foel Cwmcerwyn

This is the highest peak of the Preseli Mountains, 1760 feet high. It is sometimes called Preseli Top, which is sad, as Foel Cwmcerwyn is to my mind one of the most beautiful sounding names of any mountain: it simply rolls off the tongue.

Wales. Much of this was due to the writings of the Reverend William Gilpin, who was dedicated to the art of the Picturesque and advocated that nature needed to be improved upon. His sketches illustrated ways in which this could be done, often with complete disregard for topographical accuracy. Even so, he was full of admiration for nature: 'Nature is full of fire, wildness and imagination. Her plans are too immense for our confined optics.'

My desire to paint mountain scenery developed alongside my love for being out in the wilds. I grew up in the village of Llanddewi Velfrey, with superb views of the Preseli Mountains. Although the friendliest of hills, in winter, with a coating of snow and an angry sky, they appear forbidding. I would cycle up there occasionally and revel in the fresh gusts that blew in from the Atlantic.

I began sketching in earnest during a number of visits to the Peak District. The scenery of North Staffordshire entranced me. At first sketches were few, as I worked mainly in watercolour using a fairly large sketchbook. As I went out in all weathers I saw effects that cried out to be recorded, despite atrocious conditions. Gradually I developed all-weather techniques for watercolour sketches, at first simply shielding the sketch as much as possible with whatever was available. Light rain or snow often enhanced the work with 'happy' accidents, but wind and heavy rain proved more difficult. Why paint in rain, blizzards and gales? Because these are part of the mountain scene and lend tremendous atmosphere. Paradoxically, watercolour is the best medium to exploit these moods. Some of the most beautiful effects occur during rain or snowfall, when a pencil might fail to render the soft merging of shimmering light with background cliffs. I strive to capture the feeling of driving rain stinging the face. At times working in such conditions is so bizarre and unreal that only an advanced state of oblivious determination will provide the discipline to carry on.

One of the most lunatic attempts at sketching in watercolour occurred one afternoon after walking along the old military road from Kingshouse by the edge of Rannoch Moor to Loch Tulla. As I passed the loch an extremely heavy

Farm at Three Shire Heads

A typical gritstone farmhouse in the Peak District.

Allt a' Choire Odhair-bhig

Beyond the mountain lies Glencoe. I shivered in cold as I sketched the rickety bridge that carried the old military road from Kinlochleven to Glencoe. Lying in the pool below were the remains of a former bridge. I ended the sketch prematurely as I could hardly hold the brushes.

Snowdon from Castle of the Winds

The snow-clad peak of Yr Wyddfa (Snowdon), fire-flushed pale pink by the dying light of a February afternoon, is framed by the slate-grey splinters of frost-shattered rock on Castell-y-Gwynt (Castle of the Winds).

Collection of the author.

downpour began. I spotted a subject and got out my paints. Soon watercolour was flowing off the paper in waves, down over my wrist. It took three coats of paint before the sketch was complete, but I had the advantage then of having to run only a few hundred yards to Inveroran Hotel where I finished the sketch before leaping into a welcome bath.

Rain is usually just a nuisance, but there are times when it really goes beyond a joke. On one occasion on Snowdon I had somehow forgotten the tent, and so had to make do with an old groundsheet slung between two boulders and a makeshift stone wall. Unfortunately it was one of the wettest nights of the year. My bivouac was in Cwm Glas beneath the Parson's Nose, the butt end of a shattered ridge that climbed to Crib-y-ddysgl. It poured heavily and I felt sure that no one else would be out in such weather. Suddenly a figure appeared like some genie out of the lamp and said, 'I say, would you like a cup of tea?' I almost fell out of my sleeping bag into a muddy pool in astonishment. Apparently he was camping nearby. The tea was welcome. Next morning I awoke in a pool four inches deep, but inside my survival bag I felt snug and dry. Needless to say, it was still raining . . .

Problems abound for the wild-weather artist: brushes roll over precipices, palettes disappear into rivers, or sketches blow into muddy puddles – upside-down, of course. 'I'm saturated; exhausted by falls; my leg hurts; I've just pulled myself out of a river; the camera is jammed, and my hand has been gashed on a rock. The pack is heavy, snow is being driven into my face by gale-force winds and I can hardly put one foot in front of the other. Suddenly the mist lifts to reveal snow-clad peaks caught in sunlight. Energy flows through the veins and I leap forward like a Welsh scrum-half taking four Frenchmen over the line.' Such is the effect of morale on the physical state. It happens regularly.

High winds are particularly unwelcome. Once on the slopes of Coniston Old Man a fierce gust of wind picked me up and deposited me and sketchbook in a nearby snowdrift.

A constant source of conflict is having to decide whether to climb or sketch, for often there are times when I cannot do both owing to a lack of time. This is especially common

Pillar

This sketch shows the immense Pillar Rock, a huge buttress almost reaching the summit of Pillar Mountain on the Ennerdale side. The rock is a favourite haunt of Lakeland climbers.

during the fewer hours of daylight in winter. Sketching does slow me down considerably, which is one of the main reasons I use a tent so often. The tent also enables me to be on the heights at the crack of dawn, or watch the sun setting from some high crag – by far and away the best times of day for the landscape artist. I have never been able to drag myself out of a hotel before daybreak. Quite often, therefore, I'm heading upwards when everyone else is on the downward leg. One day, after a steady haul over Crinkle Crags in the Lake District, I climbed Bow Fell when all others had forsaken the peak. At the end of a long day in the hills I found every step needed tremendous effort. On the summit my eyes were drawn immediately to the fiery glow of the evening sky as it set the distant sea ablaze. The glow flashed violently, followed by a pouring of thick rolling mist through the gap of Mickledore, like some giant cannon between the Scafells. Had I left the hills before sunset I would have missed this glorious spectacle.

Working in the mountains during all seasons is of course not without its dangers. Even a minor ankle sprain can

Ore Gap at Sunrise
I awoke to find a sea of cloud below me, with Lakeland peaks appearing here and there, as though floating on the clouds.

OPPOSITE:
River Muick
Glen Muick is the natural approach to Lochnagar, and on a misty day when the mountain remained hidden I found the river an excellent substitute.

become a potential fatality when alone, for if one is immobilized far from the nearest road there is no one to summon help. Falling rocks, avalanches, river crossings and snow cornices giving way all add to the excitement of being in the mountains. Cold, discomfort and anxiety can seriously interfere with judgement and cumulative mistakes can be disastrous.

No matter how well equipped you are it is no guarantee that all will be well. In January 1976 two lads perished in a blizzard on Scafell Pike, despite being well-equipped. They were caught out in appalling conditions and died of exposure. It takes several expeditions to train mentally to go into a range of hostile snowy mountains alone. Having to be totally self-reliant in a hostile environment can exert powerful pressures, especially on the inexperienced. Present-day life styles are not conducive to either a self-reliant or resourceful attitude. The urge to seek shelter, move down the mountain or simply to get going when faced with the onslaught of a fierce blizzard is difficult to suppress. To stay

and sketch, in watercolour, in the face of such discomfort and at times pain, is not a natural desire. However, to ignore this aspect would be to study only the 'pretty' side of the mountain environment, which is not the dominant theme very often. Anyway, I am fascinated by the challenge of capturing nature's wilder moments.

At its best, landscape painting is very much an emotional response to the subject. Emotions can be aroused by historical association, feeling for a subject, memories, weather or companions, as much as the topography itself. Glencoe seems a much more dire place when you remember the massacre; the north-west Highlands feel far more lonely if you think of the Highland clearances; the Welsh mountains evoke feelings of mystery and legend when you have just read the *Mabinogion*, especially if it is misty. These elements can stir an artist just as much as a patch of sunlight falling out of leaden skies onto a bubbling brook.

From the sketches carried out on location I produce paintings back in the studio, endeavouring to recapture the

Pennine Sheep

*– a few of the more memorable characters
I met on my travels.*

*Swaledale tup displaying those
magnificent horns as seen on the emblem
of the Yorkshire Dales
National Park.*

*Lop-sided mop-type sheep common
around the Howgill Fells. Probably
female, but hard to tell with all that
wool.*

*Cross-looking ewe on Foxup Moor near
Plover Hill – battered and unkempt.
Despite the aggressive stance it declined
to charge.*

single badly-worn horn

tattered ear

*Curious lambs in silhouette, watching
me sketch Stainforth Bridge. Some of
them had blue jackets on, making them
look really bizarre in a sketch.*

spontaneity and mood of the moment, for without mood a painting of the mountains has no heart, and no feeling. At the same time I strive for a faithful rendition of the topography, for these are like friends whose portraits are unique. Mist and light of course can play strange tricks and even a slight change of angle or altitude can dramatically alter the perspective of a mountain. The character of a place is also important in getting a feeling for the subject.

My biggest problem in selecting illustrations for this book was what to leave out. Sadly I have had to omit many favourite subjects, but I have attempted to include a fairly representative selection of scenes. In painting the mountains one is at the mercy of the elements, not just as far as mist and rain is concerned, but in finding the right lighting. Even a mediocre subject can be transformed by dramatic lighting, and this is a matter of luck.

Cir Mhor on the Isle of Arran provided me with some of the most amazing transformations of light one morning. Firstly the mountain was caught in a strong direct patch of

Tryfan from Afon Llugwy

OPPOSITE: Cir Mhor, Isle of Arran

David Bellamy

Cairn on Cross Fell

OPPOSITE:

Blea Tarn and the Langdale Pikes

From the collection of Stuart Houghton Ltd.

David Bellamy

light, throwing it into bold relief on the Glen Rosa side. As I climbed the col to the north of the A'Chir Ridge it turned battleship grey. Dense mist descended, so I reached the pointed summit without being able to see anything but the bit of rock I stood on. However, by the time I had descended to the col below, the mist had cleared enough for me to do a further sketch. From this point Cir Mhor looked truly magnificent, coming to a sharp apex.

As an artist I am naturally concerned with the conservation of all our wild places, and particularly with those under current threat from pollution and development. The effects of acid rain on the woodlands and streams have become a cause for national concern; ugly tracks are being bulldozed across mountain-sides, seemingly without regard to the environment; skiing developments threaten the solitude, beauty and habitat of some of the Scottish hills; transport interests are cutting into Dartmoor. This is just the tip of the iceberg. Groups are forming to counter these threats, but how effective can they be when pitted against the giant developers?

However, the high mountains will never lose their wild beauty. When warm evening sunshine turns the crags red and sends patterns of light shimmering across snow-ripples on a summit ridge, and a sea of snow-clad peaks stretches to a mauve horizon, the immensity of the mountains is humbling and staggering to the lone traveller, a speck of dust on a carpet of white peaks. This is a time to savour, not to be rushing blindly home, for these moments stay in the memory when toil and pains have been forgotten.

Hark! fast by the window
The rushing winds go,
To the ice-cumber'd gorges,
The vast seas of snow!
There the torrents drive upward
Their rock-strangled hum;
There the avalanche thunders
The hoarse torrent dumb.
– I come, O ye mountains!
Ye torrents, I come!

MATTHEW ARNOLD

Roaches Farm

The mantle of winter brings a harsh backcloth to the isolated farms on the high moorland of North Staffordshire.

2
EARLY SKETCHES IN THE PEAK

The Peak District has a special place in my development as an artist, as it was here that I did much of my early work. It proved to be an excellent training ground, providing me with both gently undulating scenery and wild, exposed terrain. The first sketches varied from bad to dreadful. I used a variety of sizes of sketchbook and all the sketching materials I could lay my hands on: pencils, crayons, watercolours, pens, charcoal, pastels, bits of wood, etc. In Dimmingsdale one time I forgot my brushes and had to use tissues to push the paint around. Still, techniques had to be learned and the best way of learning is usually to make a few mistakes.

My very first serious walk was from Ashbourne up the Manifold Valley. Dove Dale and the Manifold Valley make an excellent two-day round excursion, especially in winter when the lack of people and leaves means that more can be seen. Snow fell on the cobbles of the square in Ashbourne as my companion and I set out, but it soon eased only to return in the evening to fall across the upper Manifold Valley in a beautiful moving curtain.

On that occasion we hardly saw anyone at all, and only met a couple of people on the return leg down Dove Dale the following day. The charming Dove forms the boundary between Staffordshire and Derbyshire, and was much loved by Charles Cotton and Izaak Walton, who shared common interests of angling and literature.

Padley Gorge

OPPOSITE:
Wolfscote Dale
This is the northern extension of Dove Dale, showing the dramatic limestone cliffs dropping into the River Dove.

In the south west of the district lie the North Staffordshire Moors, a particularly favourite spot of mine, and said to be the haunt of the headless horseman. During harsh winters the Roaches and Ramshaw Rocks assume truly wild proportions, the angular gritstone rocks thrusting skywards like giant upturned anvils. Farms and cottages hug the contours of the hills, seeming even more remote than usual when the landscape is under a cloak of white. On one occasion on these moors I stopped to carry out a sketch in heavy rain. The paper became saturated and messy but I then did a second sketch from the same spot. The mist lifted and without moving I was presented with yet another scene. In all, simply by turning around I completed four sketches from that one position.

If the western borders of the Peak District are dramatic in the shape of the Roaches, the eastern edges are equally so in the spectacular rock ramparts that stretch for miles above the Derwent Valley. These edges terminate the eastern moors abruptly. Above Hathersage is Stanage Edge where many old millstones lie abandoned below the cliffs. One millstone even has a birch tree growing out of the hole in its centre. Rock climbers invade these edges from all over the country and in places it is feasible for the ordinary pedestrian to scramble up fairly easy rock only a few feet from some of the really hard climbing routes. Most of my visits here have been in blustery conditions when everything needs to be held down by rocks. Many placenames hereabouts are connected with Robin Hood, and the grave of Little John is said to be in Hathersage churchyard.

Also in the eastern part of the Peak District is Padley Gorge, an especially attractive place when sunlight filters through the trees. I sat beside a pool and began a complicated painting of water, rocks, trees and shadows. Halfway through the work three teenage girls arrived, lifted up their skirts and splashed into my pool without a care for my reflections. Should I jump in with them or try to salvage what I could? Luckily they soon became bored and hopped across the rocks and out of sight.

The weather was not so kind when I decided to seek out the bridge at Three Shire Heads, where Staffordshire meets Cheshire and Derbyshire. Rain was falling but inside my cagoule I enjoyed the freshness of the windswept moors. The pouring rain enhanced the roofs of the farmhouses, causing interesting reflections. I hid behind gritstone walls to carry out sketches 'into wind' and driving rain, hoping no one in the houses would spot me lurking so suspiciously. Down by the bridges – there were two in fact – the stream was red and frothing, roaring its noisy melody. Rain still fell, but I made no attempt to shield the sketch. The rain actually seemed to improve the work. Often, however, it is the memory of the scene which matters as much as the sketch.

In the Peak District one is more likely to be distracted when sketching than in more remote regions. In Dove Dale, whilst sketching Ilam Rock, I retreated into a cave to shelter

Packhorse Bridge, Three Shire Heads
The sketch has suffered considerably from the heavy downpour which accompanied me all afternoon.

from the rain, and continued working. I was quickly joined by a troop of boy scouts and the cave became extremely congested. Before long they were singing and leaping up and down. The only way I could see my subject was to leap up and down in unison.

Another time, whilst painting Peveril Castle, I had hardly begun painting when about fifty school-children appeared. Having made the awkward climb to my vantage point they proceeded to surround me. Soon the subject was obliterated. I could only continue by pretending to pack up, and restarting when the last child had disappeared.

However, the opposite effect has also occurred; that is, when people have been eager to get away as fast as possible. I happened to be sketching in a snowstorm on top of Kinder Scout with a howling wind hurling stinging snow into my face. The effect of the Kinder River softly emerging from the deluge with its indigo waters contrasting with the snowy banks was too good to miss. With little cover available I hid in the lee of my rucksack, pushing blue snowflakes across the paper. A group of walkers appeared. They were lost and asked the way to the Snake Pass. My amusement increased as I saw the looks of utter disbelief on their faces as I sat sketching whilst giving them directions. They did not linger. On that occasion I intended camping, but my amusement soon turned to annoyance when I realized my tent pegs had been left behind. Kinder Scout in a gale is not the ideal place to try pitching a tent without pegs, so I retreated across the plateau and back to Edale.

Kinder Scout, at 2088 feet, is of course the roof of the Peak District being, like Bleaklow, an extensive plateau of peat hags and muddy channels called groughs. To me they are at their best in poor weather. Mist might make it difficult to navigate, but it usually ensures a low turn-out of walkers and often enhances the weathered rocks and groughs, giving them an air of unreality. Since the introduction of

Ilam Rock, Dovedale

Kinder River in a Snowstorm

Kinder Scout is at its most impressive when in rain with mist swirling up over the edges of Kinder Downfall like the lip of a boiling cauldron. This sketch was done in snow and sleet one March afternoon.

duck-boards on the Pennine Way section a great deal of the fun of bog-trotting has been spoilt. Much sport and merriment can be derived from seeing some poor soul go in up to his midriff, and then helping him out. Black trousers and a sense of humour are essential.

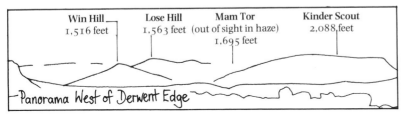

Win Hill
1,516 feet

Lose Hill
1,563 feet

Mam Tor (out of sight in haze)
1,695 feet

Kinder Scout
2,088 feet

Panorama West of Derwent Edge

Bleaklow has been called England's only desert, and how true this seems; especially after a dry spell when the wind whips up dust like a sandstorm. The black, oozing peat appears to be endless and snow transforms it to an arctic waste, hardly typical of the heart of England. Yet the place has a strange, romantic feel about it. The loneliness, the gaunt gritstone boulders and waving bog-cotton, the peat hags and cry of the curlew evoke a haunting atmosphere. Once you have experienced it you always want to go back for more.

Further east on Howden Moors the going can be really rough. My brother rashly took it into his head to join me on a

trip across this part of the Peak District. His appreciation of the need to conserve weight was sadly lacking: his rucksack appeared to be full of bottles, sauces and other cooking luxuries. Anyway, what he lacked in awareness for long-distance walking he made up for in enthusiasm, and we began at a cracking pace. The sun beat down and the sight of the Strines Inn at midday proved too tempting. We drank and drank, so that by the time we were out on the moor my navigation was not at its best. By late evening we were still well short of the Derwent.

I forged ahead through huge tufts of grass, unsure what my boots were going into. A hundred yards behind Malcolm steamed along, every now and then disappearing head-first into the kingsize grass, accompanying his fall each time with an appropriate curse. At last we reached a stream. The stove was set up on a large flat rock in mid-stream and Malcolm began preparing the soup whilst I erected the ancient tent. Thunder threatened, and as I finally had the tent up the first clap crashed overhead. The soup was ready. Unfortunately the pot in which Malcolm made the soup was unstable, and as he reached over to pour it the pot capsized and sent his delicious minestrone flowing downstream. Malcolm calmed down when I pointed out that there were at least twenty-four more packets of soup in his rucksack: nothing like

The Tower, Alport Castles

In the distance this looks like a man-made structure, but is the result of one of Britain's largest landslips.

RIGHT:
Rain Squall near Hartington

The light-coloured limestone walls of the White Peak contrast strongly with dark vegetation or stormy skies when the stone is caught in sunlight. The White Peak is so-called because the area is limestone country, as opposed to the darker gritstone of the Dark Peak.

LEFT:
Landscape near Chelmorton

Typical Peak District scenery, but beyond the distant hill lies a tormented landscape of quarries, industrial buildings and railways; a ghastly mess in otherwise idyllic countryside.

reserves. He soon cheered up when things were under way again. I prepared the inside of the tent, and then he was ready once more for my billy-can. I stood with one foot in mid-stream on a rock, eagerly awaiting Malcolm's delicious-looking brew. Alas, at the very moment he began transferring soup to my billy an incredible thunderclap rent the air, causing me to slip. This time bright red tomato and beef soup flowed away.

Some twenty-eight minutes of brewing soup to no avail did not have a very good effect on Malcolm's temper. This time it took several minutes of cajoling before another pot was under way. Halfway through the brew a downpour began, and my assurances that it was perfectly dry inside the tent did not go down very well in mid-stream. Bravely Malcolm stuck it out and only managed to spill half the soup this time, on his dash into the tent. It was a marvellous reviver and spirits improved. That, however, was the first and last backpacking trip Malcolm ever made.

Top Withens

3
BOGS AND BAGPIPES ON
THE PENNINE WAY

The Pennine Way. Those three words fired me with an unusual excitement in the early days when I began serious walking. Doing the route hooked me on the Pennines, leaving me with an insatiable desire to find out what lay on either side of that well-worn track. This chapter follows the course of the Pennine Way, to which I have returned on numerous occasions.

Kinder Groughs in Mist

Peat groughs on Kinder Scout and Bleaklow take on an eerie silence in mist when they seem to stretch interminably ahead. Kinder seems to bring out extreme reactions from walkers: some adore the place, feeling that there is nowhere quite like the summit plateau, *whilst others detest the mazelike morass of peat channels that claw your boots and stop your rhythm. This is really inhospitable terrain, and the guides warn that it should be avoided in anything but fine weather. Of course some people will go there in any conditions . . .*

Edale

After much argument as to the actual route, the footpath was officially opened in April 1965. From Edale in Derbyshire to Kirk Yetholm over the border, the Pennine Wayfarer slogs across peat hags, heather moorlands, whaleback fells and gentle dales. The record time for completing the 250 miles stands at less than three days, but of course that is done only with back-up support. The bothy book in Greg's Hut on Cross Fell reveals various attitudes to the walk, ranging from undisguised contempt for those who prefer not to make it a 'challenge in six days', to those who leisurely complete it in several trips. Far more people leave Edale, the start of the Pennine Way, than arrive at Kirk Yetholm. The peat bogs of Kinder Scout are too hard on many, so that by the time Crowden is reached the fall-out rate is high.

I began the undertaking in fine weather. Kinder Scout had no venom that day as it had on an earlier occasion when just about everything was thrown at me. Once along the western edge the path soon fell away over the northern slopes before climbing to Mill Hill, beyond which the going became distinctly boggy. At this point you start to realize who else is doing 'the Way', as there is often bunching at the boggy bits as each person takes a turn to jump across. Bleaklow comes next, stretching unrelieved to the northern horizon. By the time Bleaklow Head is underfoot the effect of several miles of oozing black peat starts to tell, both mentally and physically. But there is much more to come.

Crowden Hostel was a great relief. Still, I looked forward to more mud the next day with relish. Clouds hung low over Laddow Rocks as the band of wayfarers trickled out of the

Blackstone Edge

Apparently Defoe ran into a snowstorm here one August. He found the place 'a fearful precipice', a typically timid response from eighteenth-century travellers.

hostel and climbed towards Black Hill. The omens were not good. On the climb from Crowden I passed three people drying out after being sucked into the insidious slime up to their waists.

Black Hill is awful. The approaches are treacherous, through glutinous mud ready to swallow up the unwary. In places the ground wobbles like a giant black jelly. The summit stands at 1908 feet and is decorated by a brilliant white ordnance column, stark against a sea of black peat. The wind whipped up a minor dust-storm which affected my accuracy in setting a compass-bearing for the next part of the route, so adding a couple of miles to my journey at the blink of an eye. I soon found more black jelly on Wessenden

Moor. After that Blackstone Edge with its chaos of rocks provided a welcome contrast to the miles of boggy moorlands to the south. I continued to Mankinholes over easy terrain. North of the Calder Valley the route rises and falls steeply, in places squeezed between gritstone walls, at times crossing pleasant streams as at Colden Water with its stone footbridge. Here I lingered for lunch, sketching and basking in glorious sunshine, and joined by some of the other Pennine Way addicts.

Across Heptonstall Moor I trudged, then climbed to Top Withens, the setting that Emily Brontë is thought to have had in mind when she wrote *Wuthering Heights*. It is hard to imagine the place on a calm day, for the building seems to

Mankinholes

I stayed the night at Mankinholes Youth Hostel, to be awakened the next morning by the most dreadful din. The warden had a novel way of arousing hostellers by playing a badly-worn record of bagpipe music at full blast. I sat rather dazed on the bottom bunk when suddenly a figure whistled past my head from the top bunk, and managed a two-point landing on the floor. It was a septuagenarian cyclist who then proceeded to somersault his way round the room, much to the amazement of the other inmates. Finally, he cleaned his teeth whilst doing press-ups. His energy made my effort of walking the Pennine Way seem to pale into insignificance.

The Long Drag *is a flagged path stretching from Mankinholes to Stoodley Pike, built to provide jobs during the cotton famine.*

have been sited to obtain maximum blast from the north wind screaming up the eastern slopes of Withens Heights. From the lonely setting on high moorland I descended to the rambling old seventeenth-century farmhouse of Ponden Hall. It offered refreshments and accommodation. I welcomed the luxury of a night there after roughing it across boggy moors. It presented an opportunity to exchange experiences with other wayfarers, and of course was of no little interest for its Brontë associations, being supposedly the Thrushcross Grange of *Wuthering Heights*.

The next section to Gargrave passed quietly. Gargrave, however, was full to the brim and had no spare accommodation, so I spent the night shivering in the back of a lorry. At daybreak I continued as far as Malham where I paused to do some exploring. Malham Cove is one of the great spectacular features of the Pennines. What a shame that the waterfall no longer cascades over the top, for in spate it would have been an amazing spectacle, higher than Niagara. The stream actually creeps out of a narrow slit at the base of the 300-foot cliffs. The change in scenery here is dramatic. Gone are the heather moors and gritstone outcrops, and in their place are short grasses and light-coloured limestone. Even on a wet, gloomy day the light in this area has a strange luminosity that seems to be reflected off the rocks.

Hebble Hole Bridge

OPPOSITE:

Pen-y-Ghent and Dale Head Farm

Malham Tarn, Fountains Fell, then another highlight: Pen-y-Ghent. We queued to climb the rocky nose up the fell, the upper reaches shrouded in mist. Route-finding was quite straightforward, even in mist, and as the climb from Dale Head Farm was less than 900 feet it did not take long to reach the summit. How I wished I had more time to explore, but it was getting late and a hot meal awaited me in Horton in Ribblesdale.

Unrelenting rain accompanied me out of Horton next day. Large pools blocked the path and the roar of brownish-yellow streams crashing into potholes was fearful. By the time I approached Ling Gill Bridge my vocal chords were amply lubricated by the drizzle. Well into the second verse of 'Cwm Rhondda' I turned to cross the bridge, only to find fourteen bodies sheltering behind the parapet. I don't know who was most surprised. Beyond lay open moorland, followed by Hawes, Hardraw and the slog up Great Shunner Fell. After all those peat hags Thwaite and Keld were like oases. Before leaving Keld I did some sketching on the Swale, one of my favourite Yorkshire rivers. So late did I tarry that I left little time to reach Tan Hill Inn before afternoon closing. My pace quickened when the inn came into view, my only burst of speed along the Pennine Way, apart from an encounter with a bull in Teesdale. Tan Hill Inn is the highest pub in England at 1732 feet, and was originally built for miners and packhorse teams. Then came Sleightholme Moor, the largest mass of runny porridge I have ever crossed. After lunch, including a few pints of best ale, the porridge was tackled with a distinct lack of reverence. When I emerged the far side of the moor I must have looked as though I had just lost an argument with an agricultural muckspreader.

Cottage near Ponden Hall

High Force

The immense power of the falling Tees is awesome as it drops into a foaming pool seventy feet below: or as Viscount Torrington, an eighteenth-century explorer, said, 'about 69 feet'.

The sketch shows a classic error: I began by washing in the sky, and suddenly realized that I was halfway down the page and had not yet started work on the falls, the reason for doing the sketch. In the end it appears to run off the paper. Perhaps the ideal position to view High Force would be dangling from a rope halfway below this viewpoint and the river.

Once across the Stainmore Gap, one of the main routes used by the English and Scots to raid each other in times gone by, the River Tees was eventually reached at Middleton-in-Teesdale. The next section of the Way proved to be an absolute delight, with pleasant meadows and many rare plants. The Tees itself changes character many times, here smoothly flowing over a wide bed, there tumbling over chiselled dolerite, or squeezed into a narrow rocky defile. Higher upstream were mountain pansies, seeming incongruous in such a wild habitat. Then came the roar of water tumbling with abnormal power. This was High Force, one of the most impressive waterfalls in the country. The

River Tees

Birkdale

RIGHT:

High Cup Nick

This is a jolt to the senses after the unsensational moorland scenery since Birkdale. It suddenly hits the walker, a U-shaped valley with plunging vertical sides that look as though they have been chiselled out by some giant.

BELOW RIGHT:

Greg's Hut

This old building stands amidst disused mine-workings high on the northern flank of Cross Fell. It was renovated by the Mountain Bothies Association and the Greg's Hut Association, being named after John Gregory who died in the Swiss Alps. As I began sketching it was a signal for the full fury of the north wind to unleash itself upon me, bringing a wild snowstorm with it.

rocky gorge at this point formed a natural amphitheatre, emphasizing the noise of crashing water, and hitting the senses in a spectacular display of sound and vision.

The next major feature was Cauldron Snout where the Tees cascades over 150 feet down a rocky staircase, foaming cream, white and ochre. I stood in gale-force winds to sketch the cataract, frozen and battered, putting verticals where horizontals should go and sometimes missing the pad altogether as the wind carried it away. The first sketch I did of Cauldron Snout was many years ago. I am fairly familiar with Upper Teesdale, but puzzled long over which particular view was depicted in Turner's painting *Chain Bridge Over the River Tees*. Eventually I suspected that it must be Cauldron Snout, a suspicion confirmed in David Hill's excellent book *In*

Turner's Footsteps. But as the author points out, it is a painting far removed from reality. Above Cauldron Snout the Way crosses the Tees and passes Birkdale, apparently the loneliest inhabited place in the old county of Westmorland. Then it follows open moorland to the immense cleft of High Cup Nick. The three wonders of Upper Teesdale, High Force, Cauldron Snout and High Cup Nick, have been created by the intrusion of dolerite into the rock strata.

I spent a night at the village of Dufton before the long climb up to Cross Fell, which began with about two hundred sheep following me, Pied Piper fashion, all bleating at once. Soon they were left behind me and I passed through the rambling old farm at Halsteads. Although the building appeared to be quite sound it has been uninhabited for over

twenty-five years. These days the bedrooms are used to store fodder and the dining room is a sheep-dip. Before Cross Fell the Way passes the ghastly radar and weather station on Great Dun Fell, a dreadful eyesore. At 2930 feet Cross Fell is the highest peak in the Pennines. Its summit plateau is extensive and in mist can easily cause confusion. The northern flanks are scarred with evidence of mine-workings, the open shafts a hazard in the dark or when hidden under snow. I have seen deep patches of snow here as late as June.

The next feature of particular interest is Hadrian's Wall, where the Pennine Way abandons the Pennines then crosses the great forests of Wark and Redesdale before the final section over the Cheviots and across the border. The Roman wall is still impressive despite centuries of neglect and loss of stones for use in farms and buildings. That part of the wall east of Crag Lough to Housesteads Fort is particularly interesting. Eric, my companion north of the wall, provided a continuous source of entertainment. His humour carried us through many a bad patch, although it did dry up in the heat of the July heatwave when we found no water in the Cheviots. After almost a day without water we were desperate and had to drop a long way off route until we found a burn. Like two lumbering elephants at a waterhole we drank our fill, tired but relieved. That is, until we heard the first Phantoms coming in on a low-level bombing run, their missiles exploding behind a nearby hill. Eric eventually had to retire from the walk as his feet, after several days' hard walking, resembled flagellated beetroot, incapable of further action.

The Pennine Way is unpopular with some, is grossly over-used in summer, and is rough on those inexperienced in mountain walking; but it crosses some of the grandest scenery in the country, surely a good enough reason for exploring it. Off season it can even be lonely. It is a course to be savoured not just in summer, but in winter when snow lies crisp on the black peat of Kinder Scout like cream on a Christmas pudding; when hawthorns stand gaunt and bare against a bleak moorland setting; and coarse gritstone boulders are the only shelter from a howling wind.

Pen-y-Fan from the Upper Nevadol Reservoir

4
SOUTH OF
PONTRHYDFENDIGAID

The Brecon Beacons, when seen from the Hay road, never fail to gladden the heart. However, these are deceptive mountains: they appear so friendly, and though steep in places their lack of craggy outcrops on the high peaks gives an appearance of gentle hills. Yet they are killers, in many cases because they are not taken as seriously as, say, the mountains of Snowdonia. Even so, Pen-y-Fan at 2907 feet is only a few feet lower than Cadair Idris. I have been on Cribin in a whiteout when a blizzard raged so fiercely that I could not see my feet; almost blown off the edge of Pen-y-Fan by ferocious winds suddenly gusting; and spent fifteen minutes trying to unlock the car at the Neuadd Reservoir with numbed fingers inside gloves, because of the intense cold. Such conditions are common on the Beacons in winter.

The sight of Pen-y-Fan under snow when viewed with the Upper Neuadd Reservoir in the foreground is probably the most spectacular in South Wales. I was lucky to capture it in watercolour, as no sooner had I finished sketching than it began to snow heavily, blotting out the peaks which had moments before been bathed in glorious sunshine with plumes of spindrift spiralling hundreds of feet into the blue sky.

Not every occasion has been so easy; an earlier winter I had struggled up to the Lower Neuadd Reservoir to sketch it in appalling weather. The atmosphere was electric. Beyond the reservoir the wooded slopes were cloaked in mist. Snow lay thinly on the shores, with icy slabs jutting out into the deeper dark water. Unfortunately the ideal viewpoint was looking straight into the sleet-laden gale-force wind. The only cover available was a bush half the size of a dustbin, not the cosiest of vantage points in a gale. I sketched furiously, the wind tearing at my paper, causing it to crease, tear, fold and rub against my cagoule. The result was hardly accomplished, but at least I had something down on paper. Later in the tent I hung it up to dry. With so many creases it might as well have been wrung out first.

West of the main mass of the Brecon Beacons lies the

Pontsticill Reservoir, Brecon Beacons

David Bellamy

Clydach Gorge

*This is a fine place to attempt the
Lakeland pursuit of gill-climbing, but is
not recommended for the sane individual.*

Black Mountain, the main escarpment rising out of rolling moorland and falling sharply on the north flank. One of the most dramatic views I have seen of Carmarthen Fan was on one summer evening directly after sunset, from just outside the village of Bethlehem. The sharp prows of the peaks stood out clearly against a sand-coloured background, fine detail lost in the gloom.

On a grey November afternoon I climbed to Llyn-y-Fan Fach beneath the cliffs of Bannau Sir Gaer. According to legend a farmer whilst tending his sheep saw three girls emerge from the lake. He asked one to marry him. She agreed on condition that if he struck her three times or touched her with iron she would return to the lake. After many years of happy marriage the farmer accidentally touched her with metal. His wife called all her animals and they followed her into the lake.

I began sketching. It started to snow, and quickly the watercolour became a mess, the red sandstone flutings becoming uncontrolled red streaks. I put the resulting confusion into the map case, before climbing up to the main ridge as the snow cleared. To the west varicoloured patches of sky hung between a dark, threatening cloud ceiling and moorland ridges. I walked eastwards along the edge, being quickly overtaken by another snowstorm. The effect of snowflakes swirling over the edge into the greyness became quite hypnotic, and as it cleared a gigantic kaleidoscopic effect totally disorientated me. Dark green patches of reeds, dark red runnels of sandstone seemed to move like mobile ink blots on snow, the sandstone tentacles rising skywards. At first there was nothing to give it scale and, until the snowstorm was past, the effect was extremely confusing, though fascinating. That night I set up the tent in the intense cold, looking forward to the evening meal. Alas, I had forgotten the food and had to make do with nuts and orange juice.

In the eastern part of the Brecon Beacons National Park stand the Black Mountains, whaleback ridges of rounded hills, rising to 2660 feet at Waun Fach. No craggy massif here, but one can walk for miles once on the ridges without

Devil's Bridge, Clydach Gorge

encountering any steep gradients. The valleys are a delight, particularly the Grwyne Fawr and Grwyne Fechan, providing pleasant walking. Sadly the Grwyne Fawr Valley has been overrun by conifer plantations for much of its length.

To the south, a few miles west of Abergavenny, is the Clydach Gorge. One wet autumn afternoon I decided to seek out the Devil's Bridge, and although not dressed for the part – I had on a new pair of trousers – I did not envisage any difficulties. However, to get the optimum viewpoint meant lowering myself over vertical rocks above a foaming, churning cauldron of angry water. As I had no rope with me I decided to explore possibilities downstream. By a circuitous route I managed to reach the river about three hundred yards below the bridge. The undergrowth became too dense, so I had to resort to jumping in the river and wading across. Even in darkest Gwent – it was gloomy, raining and with almost a complete canopy of trees above – one hesitates to remove one's trousers even in the cause of art. I hitched up the bottoms of my new trousers, but halfway across they slipped down. On the far bank I walked some way along until forced to wade up in mid-stream, cross to a mud-bank and clamber up a huge unstable pile of driftwood. Briars and branches tore at me, so that by the time I stood precariously at the top of the driftwood I resembled something out of *Robinson Crusoe*. So much for my new trousers. Before me, in perfect alignment up the rocky gorge, stood the Devil's Bridge. In semi-darkness I sketched rapidly in watercolour.

Then the inevitable happened: the skies opened up and a deluge drenched the sketch. Colour ran in all directions. I rescued it as best I could perched awkwardly above the menacing dark water, trying to shield the work and looking like an Arab searching for a camel-spider in his jellabah. I gave up when it got too dark to see the subject, but at least I did not leave empty-handed.

To the north of the Brecon Beacons are the Eppynts, high moorland mainly given over to army firing ranges. Red flags fly continuously, and evidence of military presence can be gleaned from the titles of some of my paintings of this area: *The Brecon Beacons from Observation Post 15* and *Summit of Moelfre with Rocket*. Even the sheep have WD markings on their backs, as I found one glorious spring morning when the whole valley came alive with lamb bleatings. Great blue unmistakeable WD letters. A feature of this part of Wales is the beautifully cut hedgerows, so well laid they could stop a midge, let alone a sheep. The landscape would be far richer if such care were taken all over the country.

Brecon Beacons from the Drovers' Arms

This sketch was carried out on a glorious spring evening from the Drovers' Arms on the Eppynt Mountains. The old inn is now abandoned to the army and the sheep.

OPPOSITE:

Carreg Cennen Castle

The castle stands dramatically on a 300-foot limestone cliff. Beneath it is a cave in which are said to lie the cloaked figures of Owain Llawgoch and his followers, awaiting the call to come to the country's aid. Owain Llawgoch – Owen of the Red Hand – was said to have wounded his hand whilst crusading in France. Catherine, my four-year-old daughter, was terrified of the place, so we retreated, finding no cloaked figures. The castle was probably built in the twelfth century by Lord Rhys of Dinefwr. It lies on the western fringe of the Black Mountains.

Pysgotwr River

In 1854 George Borrow did not appear to be impressed by Pontrhydfendigaid. Apparently there was much mire in the street, immense swine lay in the mire and women in Welsh hats stood in the mire. South of Pontrhydfendigaid, the Bridge of the Blessed Ford, lies some marvellous, wild scenery. August is not my favourite time to go camping in the mountains. There are too many people and even more midges. Still, I decided to brave both in an attempt to explore this part of mid-Wales. I left Soar Chapel near Llyn Brianne one evening and hiked along one of the green roads towards Ty'n-y-cornel. The chapel is a lonely building in the heart of the moors and during the summer months a number of services are held there. It stands at a crossroads of green roads which make walking easy, and a fine pace can be maintained. That night, as I pitched the tent the midges struck and, sadly, on a beautiful evening I had to retreat inside to eat the evening meal, bitten in scores of places.

A hazy morning. I sketched the youth hostel at Ty'n-y-cornel, then watched a buzzard fly lazily overhead further up the valley. I turned into the valley of the Pysgotwr Fawr. It grew hotter. Soon I came upon a large herd of Welsh Blacks and watched closely for any signs of a bull. Sure enough, there he was, 150 yards away, ambling along. In my youth I recall being chased by Welsh Black bulls, ferocious creatures, and although this one was accompanied by a herd of cows I was not in a trusting mood. The bull looked up. My pace quickened. What would I do if it charged? My pack was

Pysgotwr Gorge

This is an amazing cleft in the mid-Wales landscape where steep cliffs, almost sheer in places, drop down to the rocky bed of the Pysgotwr Fawr.

OPPOSITE:

River Towy

This point is just over a mile downstream from Llyn Brianne, the river tumbling over massive boulders which at some time in the past have come crashing down from crags on the slopes above. Even after months of drought the river was still fast flowing. Hidden in the tree-clad cliffs high above the bank on the right is Twm Sion Catti's cave. Twm Sion Catti was allegedly a kind of Welsh Robin Hood.

heavy, and I suppose my only hope would have been to climb a tree. My pace became even brisker. The bull followed, but not very quickly. Gradually I drew away from the herd and thankfully slipped through a gate.

I lunched beside the Pysgotwr River, and after a sketch had a leisurely dip in the cool, refreshing water. Before joining the Towy the river cuts through a wild and spectacular gorge, its sides plunging down steeply to the river. There is no footpath, just amazing, rugged scenery. Further downstream the river meanders pleasantly through trees and meadows, chattering over a stony bed. With evening sunlight filtering through the trees I once more strode down another green lane.

I cannot leave South Wales without mentioning my native hills, the Preseli Mountains. Over the years they have given me some wild moments. These are hills steeped in the mists of Celtic legends, and appear in the *Mabinogion*, a collection of classic Welsh folk tales. The ubiquitous King

Glanrhydfach Cottage

Typical of the traditional Pembrokeshire cottages, this one lies in the heart of the

Preseli Mountains near Mynachlogddu. Sadly, many of these cottages are being pulled down to make way for new development.

Arthur is said to have chased Twrch Trwyth, a monstrous boar, across the Preseli range. In the great bowl of Cwm Cerwyn the boar turned to do battle with Arthur's host. Twrch slew eight of Arthur's champions, followed by four more the next day. The boar with a following of pigs was then chased all over South Wales, and was last seen heading out to sea off the Cornish coast.

Even in bright sunshine the Preseli Mountains can take on an eerie, mysterious air. One summer day I walked up Foeldrygarn from the Eglwyswrw side, with a powerful smell of gorse on the lower slopes. There was no wind as I began climbing the gentle incline. Suddenly, ahead of me and slightly to the left, a small tree began to shake violently, as though some giant, invisible hand was trying to tear it from its roots. Yet the air was calm all around. It was a strange phenomenon that, as I approached, stopped as suddenly as it had begun.

When clad in mist these hills are even more mysterious. Climb up Carn Meini and wend your way through the jagged rocky outcrops. Near the top is a large wedge of rock as high as a barn, beside which is a rock table. It does not need much imagination to envisage cowled figures huddled round the slab table, or hear the clash of the swords of Arthur's hosts.

David Bellamy

Carn Meini

Rock Table, Carn Meini

Fresh snow lay on Carn Meini, one of the most interesting of the Preseli summits, whilst a further snowstorm approached from the south. No birds, no sheep, no ponies – no life stirred at all, which was unusual for Carn Meini. This hill was the source of the Stonehenge bluestones.

Mist near Princetown

From the collection of Jean M Thomas.

5
BOG-TROTTING ON DARTMOOR

Nowhere have I experienced such a strong feeling of the ancient past than on Dartmoor. An atmosphere of powerful historical associations lies brooding among the stone circles, haunting the lonely menhirs, cairns and crosses that are scattered across the moor. Even the tors at times appear like mediaeval fortresses, their ramparts swarming with the fluorescent orange and blue tunics of twentieth-century walkers, come rain or shine.

It is easy to get lost on the moor, even in good weather, as many of the features are similar. Hence it is ideal terrain for learning to navigate. One hot summer day I was chased across the northern moor by a young blonde. Needless to say I did not put much effort into getting away from her. However, she only wanted to know where she was, so my hopes of an interesting afternoon were dashed. The poor girl had run about half a mile across rough ground to catch up with me, whilst a dozen of her friends, mainly male, lounged unchivalrously on the grass some distance away.

Navigation on the moor naturally becomes a trifle more difficult when mist descends. In mist and darkness, as I found myself on one occasion, it becomes ghastly. Of course I should never have allowed myself to get into that situation, but time and place have a habit of being forgotten when engrossed in a watercolour. The only indication then that I am in the middle of a bog is when the ground starts to move about or my knees disappear. However, there are times when Dartmoor mists have given me some of the most superb subjects I've ever seen. Princetown is covered in mist fairly regularly, and with a pale winter sun filtering through the vapour, causing a sparkle on the snow, it is a scene hard to beat. On the tors the stern granite shapes almost assume living, reptilian qualities, metamorphosed by swirling mist.

Dartmoor is perhaps at its best in foul weather, something I feel it has in common with Kinder Scout in Derbyshire. It is no coincidence that when it starts raining on the moor my sketchbook is out far more often than when

Moon Rising above Hay Tor

A sketch done on a frosty November evening. Behind me a sea of ridges and tors undulated in silhouette against the fiery glow of a dying sunset. Gone were the crowds. Dartmoor was at its most magical.

Hound Tor from Hayne Down

Evening light catches one of Dartmoor's most majestic tors. My first visit to Hound Tor took place in dense mist, when I ran into an eight-foot monster with a reptilian head the size of an armchair. It took me aback at first, until I realized it was a Dr Who monster. The film crew were round the far side of the tor.

Clapper Bridge, Powder Mills

the sun is shining. At the Powder Mills, site of a former gunpowder factory, I rattled off three watercolour sketches in rapid succession during a particularly heavy downpour. I ran out of hands to hold them and all three studies were soon in quite a mess. This was further fouled up by having to insert them into my map case; not easy with limp sheets of paper. Wet watercolour, when squeezed tightly between two flat surfaces, is highly unpredictable and produces many accidents, most of them awful. Some people have commented, however, on how it has improved the work.

On a later walk near Swincombe I was inspired by a house on the moor, in the middle of the usual downpour. I managed a quick drawing, and then tried to get it into the map case. The wind would have none of it. The last two inches refused to be pushed in, so out it all came again. A gust tore the paper from my hand and it landed on the far side of a barbed-wire fence. I reached through, caught the sketch, but scratched myself doing so. The map case became entangled in the barbed wire. With one hand it took several

minutes to disentangle myself before the process of inserting the muddy drawing into the map case began again. It became badly folded and extremely difficult to move either way, so there was nothing for it but to remove the entire contents and reinsert them all together. At last the sketch was safe, but it had taken fifteen minutes to put away and only four to sketch. After this experience I constructed a plastic folder in which to insert damp sketches, but it still created a mess.

One frosty November morning I left the car near Gutter Tor and headed towards Nun's Cross Farm, a solitary building in the heart of the southern moor. From here I continued to Fox Tor. As I approached the tor a fox rose out of the bracken and ran off, its brilliant ruddy coat glistening in the sunlight. Dartmoor is the one place in Britain where I regularly see foxes. Near Fox Tor lies Childe's Tomb, scene of a macabre tale. Childe the hunter was caught in a snowstorm whilst hunting. He slew his horse and disembowelled it so that he might shelter in its carcass, and was found some time later frozen to death. I turned south for some distance, then came upon what appeared to be a standing stone silhouetted directly below the sun. The juxtaposition of sun and stone intrigued me, so I carefully sketched the scene. Pleased with my effort, I packed up and continued past the 'stone', which turned out, to my amazement, to be an old railway sleeper sticking out of the ground. I tore up the sketch in disgust, wondering why on earth anyone would want to plant a railway sleeper in such an inaccessible part of the moor. Why plant one at all?

Eventually I reached my next target, Huntingdon clapper bridge. One of my early fascinations with Dartmoor was its clapper bridges, and I've spent many happy hours seeking them out. William Crossing's *Guide to Dartmoor* has been a great help in this respect. Although first published in 1909 it is still the most useful book on the moor. Crossing seems to

Lether Tor
Rising dramatically out of the surrounding moor high above Burrator

Reservoir like a granite castle, Lether Tor was caught by the late afternoon sunshine.

North from King's Tor

Dartmoor Ponies

Dartmoor Mist

The drystone walls of the moor are unmistakeably Dartmoor. Great use has been made of massive granite boulders, and the manner in which these have been integrated with the wall systems is ingenious.

have spent a great deal of time meticulously measuring and recording many of the crosses, stones and bridges. In his day one of the horizontal slabs of this clapper had fallen into the river, apparently caused by a flood. Happily, it has been restored.

At Huntingdon Cross I turned west along the Abbot's Way, a mediaeval route which runs from Buckfast Abbey to Buckland and Tavistock Abbeys, and is marked by granite crosses for much of the way. Beyond Red Lake it began to get dark and I felt for the comforting shape of my torch in the rucksack as I completed another sketch. Alas, the only comforting shape there was the spare battery for the non-existent, forgotten torch. I managed a weak grin and resumed the walk at the double. Sheepstor appeared ahead, a silhouette in the fading light; well worth a sketch. I did not dare put anything down on the ground, as I would never have found it again. A quick drawing was done, and then I charged off down to the River Plym and waded across. At this stage I caught sight of the moon, stopped in my tracks and got a boot full of water for my pains.

Across the Giant's Basin at Ditsworthy Warren I came upon the enormous Drizzlecombe standing stone. With the moon behind it it was even more evocative than my sleeper in the sun, and called out for a sketch. By this time it was

LEFT:
Tavy Cleave

This huge cleft in the western edge of the moor affords a delightful walk beside the bubbling Tavy, leading eventually into the heart of the northern moor. High up on the left is Ger Tor.

From the collection of Mr and Mrs Phil Davis.

RIGHT:
Fingle Bridge

The perimeter of Dartmoor is ringed by many delectable valleys, and here the Teign cuts through a charming wooded vale before turning south.

impossible to see what colours I was using, so I hoped the work would not look too sick in the morning light. Then came the final leg of the walk, across rough terrain: large boulders hidden in bracken and heather, with only faint moonlight and the glow from the lights of Plymouth to steer by. Luckily I found no bogs and, apart from one or two tumbles, I managed to reach the car without mishap.

Dartmoor bogs have perhaps been exaggerated ever since the days of *The Hound of the Baskervilles*, and most constitute more of a nuisance than any real hazard. They are usually betrayed by the brilliant green sphagnum, and can

thus be avoided fairly easily. At times I suddenly realized that the ground I was standing on was wobbling alarmingly for some eight feet or so in all directions. It was not a pleasant feeling and at any moment I expected to sink into some murky depths to the accompaniment of rising sulphurous mists. I did see one farmer's son plunge head first into a deep morass as he rode a trail bike across the moor. He quickly extricated himself whilst I hauled his bike out. His father then rode up on an All Terrain Vehicle which sported three huge ballon-like wheels – ideal for rounding up sheep on Dartmoor. In February the boggy areas are often alive with

Stone Circle, Erme Plains

This stone circle stands at the southern end of one of the longest stone rows in the country, over two miles long.

Bowerman's Nose

This peculiar outcrop is said to be named after Bowerman the Hunter who was turned to stone by a host of evil witches, together with his pack of hounds. From the north east the Nose appears like a squat totem.

Sunset over Pew Tor

frogs, and in Taw Marsh I recall seeing one contented female sliding down a trickle of water with four or five males clinging tenaciously to her back.

The moor has been called the 'last wilderness of southern England', but for how much longer will it remain a wilderness? In common with other areas of natural beauty it is constantly being threatened. The decision to route the Okehampton bypass to the south of the town has meant that a considerable slice of the National Park has tragically been lost for ever. To tear a chunk out of Dartmoor is particularly invidious, for not only is the moor one of our smallest National Parks, it is the only one in southern England. Sadly, conservation of the most beautiful parts of the country does not appear to be a prime consideration of the government.

Misty Day, Tarn Hows

6
FELLS AND TARNS

Snow lay crisp on the tops. Looking up, the eastern slopes of Coniston Old Man seemed deceptively easy, and at first the climb provided no problems. It was a joy to be out on such a clear, sunny morning. Over the snow-line I followed the miners' track past abandoned mines. Low Water was frozen solid. The going became more strenuous as the snow deepened. I passed a couple arguing furiously about the wisdom of continuing without ice-axes. She was eager to get to the top, whilst fifty feet below he stood terrified. I had no ice-axe either. This world of winter mountains was new to me and I wondered if I was doing the right thing. I soon found out.

The next slope had less snow and was terrifyingly slippery; a convex slope that disappeared somewhere below.

Approaching Rain, Thirlmere

One slip and I would slide off, gathering speed until I probably smashed myself on rocks hundreds of feet below. A sobering thought. An ice-axe would arrest such a fall. Holds had to be kicked all the way up; precarious holds that could mean life or death. There was nothing for my hands to grip except an occasional rock. This was probably the most stupid risk I would ever take in the mountains. If I survived this, I thought, the first thing I must do is get an ice-axe. With the grace of a hippo on an ice-rink I inched my way towards the summit, each kick potentially a fatal slip. I reached the top thankfully, and then followed the main ridge of the Coniston Fells, enjoying sketching in the sunshine. In every direction there were glorious views.

I turned left for Grey Friar and down over rough ground to Seathwaite Tarn which was partly iced over, then put on a spurt to get down into Dunnerdale. Dusk fell as I crossed the Duddon and headed along a track beside Grassguards Gill. Reaching Eskdale before it became completely dark was now a forlorn hope. I stumbled along, barely able to see the path, let alone navigate across the open fell. Beyond the forest I climbed higher, half considering a retreat, for heaven knew what lay ahead. It was almost pitch black, but without a tent or sleeping bag there was no stopping, however dark it became. On cresting a hill my concern turned to joy as I caught sight of the moon rising in an inky sky. Gradually the route became easier to follow as the moonlight grew brighter. Dim shapes of distant fells appeared. It was magical. My tiredness had evaporated; the moon had infused me with new strength. I felt a tinge of regret on arriving at the road below Hardnott Pass, and made my own way down the dale to the youth hostel.

It was not so calm when I headed off for Scandale Head one winter day. At High Sweden Bridge, a popular subject with photographers, I carried out my last sketch in comparative comfort. Up the walled track to the Scandale Pass I ran into the teeth of a ferocious, icy wind. Higher up the valley I abandoned the snow-covered track. The wind increased in intensity. My route lay in a horseshoe pattern, so on reaching the ridge ahead I could turn west and away from the headwinds. However, gaining the crest was slow and energy-sapping. I could scarcely manage five or six steps at a time through thigh-deep snow, although the wind would have knocked me over constantly had I not been so well anchored. Although the sun appeared at frequent intervals, ahead the sky was exceptionally black. Spindrift stung my eyes and made my jaw sore, but eventually the gradient eased. I worked my way westwards, my face at last out of that infernal wind. Here the snow lay hard and easy to walk on without crashing through. Frozen snow-ripples and snow-mushrooms as large as dining tables, sculpted by the wind, formed amazing patterns. Coniston Water glittered in the distance. Further down the ridge tall plumes of spindrift rose into the sky above High Pike. Sketching in such strong winds was horrendously difficult, but I managed a few quick studies. The Scafells, Crinkle Crags, Bow Fell and the Langdale Pikes carved a fascinating panorama to the west. Beyond High Pike some sheep were pitifully pawing the snow in an endeavour to find some food. After a few tumbles in deep snow I passed Low Pike and returned to High Sweden Bridge.

One of the first mountains I climbed in Lakeland was Helvellyn, probably because I had heard of Striding Edge and was eager to see what it was like. Unfortunately mist dogged the upper sections of the route, although it cleared at times to reveal Red Tarn nestling below the eastern precipices of Helvellyn. Striding Edge proved to be exhilarating. Here in April 1803 Charles Gough fell several hundred feet towards Red Tarn during a blizzard. Apparently over two months later when his body was found, it was still guarded by his faithful Irish terrier. Striding Edge vies with Sharp Edge on Blencathra for the most exciting ridge in the Lake District. I feel that Sharp Edge is slightly more thrilling.

From Helvellyn summit the path descending to Swirral Edge, the other arm forming the corrie of Red Tarn, was hidden in mist below a steep convex slope. Happily the mist cleared long enough for me to catch sight of the route. Down by the tarn I sketched the corrie until my teeth chattered with cold. The work was packed prematurely into my

Below Zero at Stickle Tarn

*The tarn was partly iced over, and despite
strong sunshine I shivered. Ahead,
Harrison Stickle dominates the tarn,
whilst to the right is the craggy façade of
Pavey Ark.*

rucksack and I headed at full speed for the warmth and comfort of Glenridding.

When I first climbed Scafell Pike it was in dense mist, so when on a later occasion mist hung over the fell again I resolved to climb and stay up there until it cleared, even if it took days. First I would try Scafell. However, on arriving at the foot of Lord's Rake, a switchback gully across the north face of Scafell, the mist had departed. After much slipping and sliding I found the summit bathed in warm sunshine. My descent led down into Deep Gill, a fearful chasm that looks more horrifying than it actually is, and is worth negotiating for the tremendous rock architecture. Although it was midsummer, a patch of snow lay in the innermost recesses. Soon I stood on Mickledore, the col between Scafell and Scafell Pike, at 3206 feet the highest mountain in England. It was here in 1802 that the poet Coleridge, who must have been one of the earliest fell-walkers, descended Broad Stand, a short but tricky climb. He had several other adventures before reaching safety.

I stayed awhile on the summit, a sea of stones sur-

Sharp Edge

An exhilarating arete high above Scales Tarn on the eastern ramparts of Blencathra. There were several people on the ridge on this occasion, so it was no problem to wait for the opportunity to include one in the sketch.

Deep Gill, Scafell

On the right is Scafell Pinnacle where Owen Glynne Jones climbed with the Abraham brothers in the late 1890s. Ashley and George Abraham were photographers and so the problems of climbing were complicated by the need to pose halfway up a rock face. Jones, on being asked to 'step out a foot or two', declared emphatically that to do so would involve stepping a few hundred feet into Deep Gill, an action for which he had not made adequate preparation.

rounded by some of the roughest country in the Lake District. Then I dropped down to the head of Piers Gill, erecting a tent in an idyllic spot beside the stream which plunges into the gill. Across the valley the magnificent south face of Great Gable stood rose-tinted in the evening sunshine. Great Gable, though only 2949 feet high, has been called the grandest mountain in the Lake District. It is certainly imposing and featured strongly in the emergence of rock-climbing as a sport, rather than as a method of climbing mountains, when Haskett Smith made the first ascent of Napes Needle in 1886. Its most interesting aspect is the upper part of the south face where the Napes Ridge stands proud, defined on either side by wide scree gullies. After a morning of sudden showers each time I opened my sketch-book, my luck took a new twist. As I left Sprinkling Tarn to pick up the south traverse which runs directly across the

Scafells Panorama

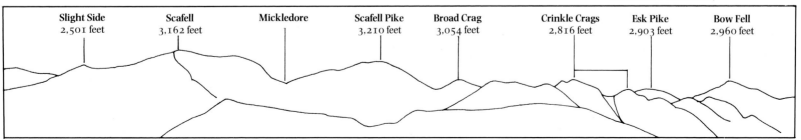

Slight Side	Scafell	Mickledore	Scafell Pike	Broad Crag	Crinkle Crags	Esk Pike	Bow Fell
2,501 feet	3,162 feet		3,210 feet	3,054 feet	2,816 feet	2,903 feet	2,960 feet

Great Gable from Sprinkling Tarn

Cove Beck Bridge and Brown Pike

south face, angry clouds rolled back, their place taken by warm October sunshine. The traverse is a walkers' route passing the foot of the Napes Ridge, where several interesting rock features stand. Almost every viewpoint demanded a precarious position: no problem when climbing or traversing the face, but when sketching I tend to forget where I am after the first minute or so, and am liable to fall off unless hooked to a rock.

Apart from one or two awkward moments the session passed uneventfully. The sunshine made it a pleasant interlude, the views across to the Scafells and down to Wast Water were breathtaking, and my craggy surroundings completed a scene of utter wildness. There followed an arduous climb up Little Hell Gate, the scree slope forming the western limit of the Napes. On attaining the final ridge which led to the summit I gazed down at the impressive sight of Tophet Bastion, the eastern buttress of the ridge. Two climbers appeared like coloured ants at the top of the buttress, linked by a thread. The sun was now falling through a deep purple sky between two peaks. After a brief pause on the summit I shot down the western scree slopes towards Beck Head at breakneck speed, almost tearing open the seat of my trousers in the process.

What a different picture the Gable presented next day. From the Dore Gap threatening weather could be seen hovering over Great Gable and the Scafells. By the time I had reached the summit ridge of Red Pike a snowstorm was coming in from the east. Excitedly I sketched at top speed. Each peak was blotted out in turn. There was barely enough time to include the jagged foreground rocks as the blizzard hit me. What a change in the weather, and it was only mid-October. Later in the afternoon on the summit of Pillar Mountain the storm still raged. I had a violent disagreement with my compass, and only after making an ass of myself on a steep rock face did I concede to its superior capability. Below the mist Ennerdale loomed dark and sinister, the stark rock forms etched deeply against a fading silver light. Black Sail youth hostel was a welcome sight, even if overcrowded.

There are blizzards and blizzards. The one on Red Pike

Napes Ridge, Great Gable
Viewed here from the Corridor Route

was benign compared with that on the Coniston Fells one icy February day. The forecast was bad, and looking at the sky I would not have argued with the prediction. Undeterred, I left Torver, near Coniston, and climbed the track beside Cove Beck. The going was easy, over crackling, frosty ground. I paused to sketch Cove Beck Bridge with Brown Pike in the background and icicles in the foreground, the stove firing away simultaneously. Alas the resulting soup was not very warm and the washes on my sketch were reticulating in the cold. I was glad to be under way again, heading directly for

Goat's Water, a tarn locked in the wild amphitheatre between Dow Crag and Coniston Old Man. The upper part of Dow Crag was wreathed in mist and a thin sprinkling of snow lay on the ground. After hopping over the last few boulders I reached the edge of Goat's Water, which was frozen over at the far end. The picture was one of absolute wildness, with Dow Crag dominating the corrie. Hiding the tent and food between rocks, I began climbing the scree to the foot of a gully which led almost to the summit of the crag. This provided an exhilarating climb with breathtaking views downwards to the tarn, black and forbidding. Halfway up the gully the first snowflakes started to fall gently in an almost calm atmosphere. The gully gave excellent shelter

Dow Crag in Mist

Gully, Dow Crag

Seen from near the summit, looking downwards during a blizzard.

from the wind. In parts snow lay deep and loose, but higher up it became firm and more responsive to the ice-axe. Here it was more exposed. Without warning, on cresting the top I was almost thrown backwards down the gully by the sudden force of the wind. I was totally unprepared for the savage blizzard that hit me. The driving snow blinded me, forcing a retreat into the shelter of some rocks, to put on goggles and pull down the balaclava. I then headed for the summit of Dow Crag, mindful that the wind should be more or less behind me once I began descending on the far side.

Madness gripped me: I stopped to paint the upper section of a gully, with massive buttresses falling into the swirling greyness below. My feet were safely anchored in deep snow

Packhorse Bridge, Wasdale Head

and my back stood to windward. I soon became chilled. From the summit my route lay downwards to the col with Coniston Old Man. I kept as close to the edge as possible, for fear of missing the col altogether. Snow still drove hard into my face. The goggles limited visibility but at least allowed me to keep my eyes open. It took some time to reach the col and all the while I was becoming colder. I then turned right to descend to Goat's Water, only to find the fury of the storm driving full into my face. The wind was naturally funnelling up over the col. Visibility was impossible beyond a couple of yards. Suddenly I slipped and went flying, fortunately landing on my rucksack. I had slid on a solid slab of grey ice hidden under a layer of snow.

Where was the tarn? I stopped and gazed downwards. No sign of the black icy water that had been so distinct from the gully. I moved on. Then some sixth sense pulled me short. Something was wrong. I gasped for breath, my mouth choked with snow. I was about to move forward again when I realized the ground ahead was uncannily flat. Then it dawned on me: I was standing beside the tarn, about to plunge into it, unaware that it was covered in ice and snow here. With the heavy rucksack it could have been the end of me, though I had no idea how deep it was at this point. With that narrow escape I retired, having had an interesting day.

Dow Crag, Dollywaggon Pike, Swirl How, Crinkle Crags, Great Gable, Catstycam, Blencathra; evocative names that inspire glorious memories of exciting days in the hills of Lakeland. Like old friends, they are always there, and always a joy to return to, for the true mountain-lover can never tire of them.

Farm, Pott Moor

7
PEAKS AND POTS IN YORKSHIRE

Coughing and spluttering like a worn-out engine, I climbed out of Clapham hardly fit enough for the task ahead. Behind me the sun was setting beyond a line of bare trees. In front were the slopes of Ingleborough. My pace quickened as spirits rose and I fell into a comfortable rhythm. Somewhat belatedly my thoughts ran through a checklist of gear. What had I forgotten this time? Only the kettle. How on earth was I going to make a brew? Should I go back? No, it was getting dark and I could always use the shallow pan.

I aimed to camp above Gaping Gill, well situated for an early ascent of Ingleborough next morning, or perhaps that night, moon permitting. Lights flashed ahead and shadowy figures arose from out of the ground, clad in black one-piece garments, like sinister serpents seeking their prey. They hailed me and stopped to chat as yet another figure emerged from a dark slit in the rocks. Theirs was a subterranean playground, their only problem being a desperate need to get down to the village before opening time. This was caving country. Light was failing as I continued my way, guided by the roar of water crashing into Gaping Gill. I set up the tent, disappointed that there was no moon.

After an evening of planning and burning fingers on unsuitable cookpans, the next day brought an amazing pattern of weather. Usually the elements seem to work against me, as though eager to stifle any artistic endeavours, but today they could not have worked better had I orchestrated them myself. After a quick exploration of the stream disappearing into Gaping Gill I set forth up Ingleborough. This is superb walking terrain, with magnificent views. The Great Scar limestone has given the area many unusual features: Ingleborough and Pen-y-Ghent are riddled with caves and potholes; streams disappear underground with startling suddenness; hillsides are characterized by long light-coloured limestone scars, and erosion of rock on Pen-y-Ghent and Ingleborough has given them distinctive profiles.

I felt a sense of foreboding in the weather. Menacing dark clouds threatened from the north. Forever optimistic, I trudged upwards in the hope of spectacular views higher up. I glanced across the valley to Pen-y-Ghent, which looked

magnificent under a capping of snow. From the north the great whaleback ridge was quickly being swallowed up by a curtain of snow. Frantically I pulled out a sketchbook and began laying on washes of watercolour before Pen-y-Ghent became completely obliterated. The scene was electrifying. Most of the mountain was now blotted out, the huge rock buttresses at the southern end etched against a fading light,

Ingleborough from the South

seeming to rise and fall like the prow of a battleship fighting its way through a stormy sea. The colours ran into one another, for there was no chance of them drying before the next was laid. Then the storm was upon me. Snowflakes swirled from every direction, totally isolating me from the surrounding fell. I huddled up to protect the wet sketch until the blizzard passed. On reaching the ridge I had to turn directly into the storm and with visibility down to fifty yards it was not pleasant. Suddenly the storm cleared to give way to blue skies, with a brilliant white slope of virgin snow ahead. I climbed over the crest of the summit plateau, almost being hurled back by a fierce wind. I marched across to the shelter walls, noting an interesting prospect of Whernside to the north. After a couple more sketches I descended the

Gaping Gill Entrance

Gaping Gill was first explored by a Frenchman called Martel in 1895. After diverting Fell Beck he descended the vertical shaft using rope ladders, some 340 feet. Above ground the entrance looks awesome. On one occasion I arrived as the Bradford Pothole Club were starting to pack up their Bank Holiday Meet. There were still a few people underground, so I asked if they would winch me down. Five people said, 'No'. 'Couldn't I be dropped down quickly?' I enquired hopefully. 'Everyone goes down at same speed,' retorted one wag. In the end they relented and issued me with a name tag – a comforting touch – and down I went.

Gaping Gill Main Chamber

I descended into the awful depths like a human spider being lowered down the plughole with the tap full on. Wet, glistening rocks, worn smooth by centuries of falling water, shot past, inches from my nose as I gathered speed. Soon the main chamber opened out below. An orange-coloured floodlamp illuminated the murky bowels.

With a jerk I hit the stony, uneven floor, greeted the other shadowy figures and then set about sketching. The two figures in the sketch have been drawn too large in relation to the immense size of the chamber. They were washing themselves in falling water. The chamber is said to be large enough to hold York Minster.

David Bellamy

Whernside

At 2419 feet Whernside is the highest of the famous Three Peaks of Yorkshire, the others being Ingleborough (2373 feet) and Pen-y-Ghent (2273 feet). The round of the Three Peaks has become a classic walk. Here the peak is seen from Simon Fell.

Rowten Pot

This is a horrific abyss 365 feet deep on the slopes of Gragareth. Warm sunlight tinted the limestone, but below the sinister shadows looked cold and bottomless. Falling water splashed and echoed in an unseen plunge into the black void. In darkness underground falling water is amplified to a deafening, threatening roar, drawing you towards it like a magnet, yet at the same time sending waves of trepidation up your spine.

OPPOSITE:
Cottage on the North York Moors

north-east flanks to Simon Fell, where I stopped for lunch and more sketching.

Down in the Ribble Valley I found myself in scorching sunshine, and rather glad to reach Pen-y-Ghent Café in Horton in Ribblesdale to relieve a terrible thirst. I then headed for Crummackdale, to where I estimated a break to be in the limestone cliffs at the head of the dale. However, I found myself at the top of sheer cliffs with no easy route down. I decided to climb down, which with my huge rucksack was easier said than done. Holds looked adequate, and so encouraged a false sense of confidence. Finding a crack in the cliff I gingerly lowered myself into what is known as a layback stance. Holds were ample, but a layback with forty pounds on your back is excruciatingly painful on the arms. One of the cardinal rules of rock-climbing is to test

a rock before putting any weight on it. This I did, but as my whole weight came to bear on the rock it gave way, crashing into the valley below. Luckily my right hand had jammed firmly in a solid crack, so I did not fall. In fact it was so well jammed that I almost fell off in freeing it. I made my way down the crack. The sheer vertical bit was only about twelve feet high, but as I neared the shelf below my left foot jammed in a cleft. Amazingly it was somehow above my head and each passing second increased the agony. The situation called for the skill of Houdini and the agility of a Russian lady gymnast, neither of which qualities I could muster. I tried to pull myself partially up, but felt as though a ton of bricks hung from my back. Desperately I wriggled out of the rucksack straps, one arm at a time, and the sack dropped on to the shelf. This eased my problem. I hauled myself up,

extracted the foot, and swiftly climbed down, moving with the confidence of a matador until I sat on an unexpectedly sharp rock spike. Literally that brought me down to earth with a bang. I heaved on the rucksack and descended the slope below the shelf; awkward, steep, but easy. Then I found myself in the lush valley below, heading for Clapham village.

Snowstorms were also the order of the day during my first visit to the North York Moors. Beautiful atmospheric effects caused by pale sunshine glimmering through retreating snowfall occurred many times. Excellent practice for rapid sketching. Rosedale Moor, Fylingdales Moor and Westerdale Moor were each in turn transformed into snowy deserts just long enough for me to produce a sketch. The views from the highest part of the moors were extensive, and that from the summit of Hasty Bank is particularly impressive. The climb up the eastern side proved to be entertaining, as the slopes were wet and slippery. Even my new vibrams had difficulty gripping the muddy slope. One girl on her way down slid most of the way, to her companions' glee. The panorama from the top swept round the Cleveland Hills, and in the far distance tall columns of smoke betrayed the presence of Middlesbrough. The rabbits

Farm near Osmotherley

up there were adept at traversing narrow ledges, and when startled raced along at break neck speed, oblivious to the precipitous drops.

One of my favourite parts of Yorkshire is the moorland area around Haworth. Perhaps it is a sense of the history of the Brontës and their tragic lives. Matthew Arnold captures the feel of summer moors very well in his poem *Haworth Churchyard*, written after the death of Charlotte Brontë:

> Sleep, O cluster of friends,
> Sleep! – or only when May,
> Brought by the west-wind, returns
> Back to your native heaths,
> And the plover is heard on the moors,
> Yearly awake to behold
> The opening summer, the sky,
> The shining moorland – to hear
> The drowsy bee, as of old,
> Hum o'er the thyme, the grouse
> Call from the heather in bloom!
> Sleep, or only for this
> Break your united repose!

I returned to Top Withens to do some sketching and found the weather even worse than on my previous visit. This was one of the few occasions when I had an audience. Heads peered out of every aperture in the ruin, probably wondering why on earth I was scratching around in a puddle of water, and crouching in pouring rain on the open moor. I don't use an easel out of doors, so it is not normally obvious that I am sketching.

In South Yorkshire the peat moors stretch into distant planes of hazy blue-grey, relieved in places by waving white flecks of bog-cotton. At times these moors seem empty and desolate, save for the persistent trill of the skylark, and yet the walker is never far from a road or town. To some it might seem a strange place to seek painting subjects. It took me some time to come to terms with the challenge of barren moors, but if there is no obvious focal point I search for a

Storm over Wharfedale

I caught this storm as I descended the western flanks of Great Whernside towards Kettlewell.

rock, clump of heather or hawthorn to evoke a feeling of loneliness. However, these moors contain a wealth of subjects: farms, cottages and gritstone crags thrusting out of the heather. There is little shelter, but this can be a spur to work quickly, and a driving wind in the face can enliven one's response to nature.

Travelling along the old packhorse routes is a fascinating way of exploring the area, which is particularly rich in these features. In places they can no longer be seen, having been ploughed up, or are overgrown or under a new road. Traces of the tracks can be easily distinguished here and there by flagstones, packhorse bridges and waymarkers.

Packhorse Days on Blackstone Edge

The **Aiggin Stone** was possibly a mediaeval way-cross. Part of its top appears to have broken off – probably when it fell over. It has since been re-erected.

This cobbled packhorse route crosses Blackstone Edge near the Aiggin Stone and Roman Road. Before the introduction of turnpike trusts and canals in the eighteenth century, packhorses were the only workable way of carrying goods across the rough hillsides of the Pennines. Flags and cobbles were laid to give the ponies a firm footing. Galloway ponies were preferred as pack animals, and there could be thirty or more in a train. Each horse normally carried over two cwt and loads comprised of salt, lime, cloth, lead and other items.

Lydgate is an ancient farmhouse lying in the shadow of Blackstone Edge. Originally it was a packhorse inn where packhorse teams would spend the night: packmen would usually sleep with their packs in an outbuilding, whilst the animals were kept enclosed outside.

Moorland Sunset, East Bolton Moor

Farms seem to be more numerous in the Yorkshire Dales, or is it an illusion created by the incredible number of stone barns? These farms are a delight to the painter's eye. Rendering the mellow stonework is an interesting challenge. Sadly, so many farms now appear like factories, with metal towers soaring skywards, alien to the natural landscape. At Brimham Rocks, however, the atmosphere is completely natural. I arrived there as dawn was breaking. The massive gritstone rocks, sculpted by centuries of wind, ice and rain, etched dark, primaeval silhouettes against a warm glow in the eastern sky. Snowflakes started to fall and the scene began to change dramatically. I had to work quickly to capture the magical atmosphere before the sunlight was blotted out, bringing me back to reality.

The Strid

Here the River Wharfe is squeezed into a narrow sandstone defile. The force of the water has worn out treacherous underground chambers where swirling eddies and strong currents can overcome a competent swimmer. Although the jump is not wide, it has claimed many lives.

Goredale Scar

At some time this must have been a huge cavern into which the roof fell. The limestone cliffs rise to over three hundred feet and overhang in places in wild contortions. The place has excited many artists, including Turner.

Brimham Rocks at Sunrise

David Bellamy

Bridge, Llanberis Pa

8
WILDEST WALES

For over two hundred years, Snowdonia has attracted artists to a greater extent than any other part of the principality. During the Napoleonic Wars, when access to the continent was restricted, North Wales swarmed with artists and tourists. The tourists were generally timid of the mountains and liable to swoon at the slightest hint of vertical rock. The artists, including Turner, Cotman, Rowlandson and John 'Warwick' Smith, naturally made the most of every bit of vertical rock that the spectacular scenery of Snowdonia could offer. Of all the artists, however, it was perhaps David Cox who took the area to his heart, spending regular visits here. From the Carneddau in the north to Cadair Idris and the Rhinogs in the south, this region is the wildest and most rugged in Wales.

Some of the roughest terrain lies in the Rhinogs, or Harlech Dome as they are sometimes called. They are not high mountains: the highest, Y Llethr, is only 2475 feet, but what they lack in height they make up for in scenery. One summer evening I climbed the Roman Steps in Bwlch Tyddiad. The steps are not reckoned to have been Roman, but of later, mediaeval origin. Near the top of the pass I turned and gazed at the sun dying beyond steep, hazy crags. I stopped to sketch. The midges began to bite. I scratched with one hand, painted with the other. It was torture. Down came my balaclava and sleeves buttoned at the wrist, but still they persisted. I sketched, scratched and hopped. Eventually I retired to erect the tent in the dark. One of my hopes was to locate the wild goats and sketch them. I had no

Roman Steps, Bwlch Tyddiad

Feral Goats

On the right is the sensational ridge on Rhinog Fach above a point where it drops down to Llyn Hywel.

OPPOSITE:
Llyn y Cau

The cliffs of Craig y Cau are caught in early morning sunshine.

idea what my chances were of spotting them. Imagine my surprise when I flung back the tent-flap next morning to find a herd of the goats trailing past the tent in single file. Clad only in Y-fronts, I grabbed a sketchbook and hared off in pursuit. Luckily I didn't see anyone, though it didn't necessarily follow that no one saw me. Later on the goats had their own back by spying on me swimming in a lake.

The next time I swam in a lake was in Llyn y Gadair on Cadair Idris. The morning grew so hot that I threw down my sketchbook and jumped into the lake. Afterwards, as I dried out on the warm rocks two American girls appeared and asked me if I was madman or poet. Possibly my near nudity on a bare mountainside provoked the query, or perhaps American girls are slightly more original and daring with

Cottage near Dolgellau

their opening lines. Anyway, according to legend anyone who spends the night on Cadair Idris will by morning be a madman or poet.

Lazily, I hauled myself up the precipitous Cyfrwy Ridge. About halfway up stands a conspicuous rock 'table' – Idris's Table. Above this I negotiated the unstable ridge to a spot that afforded a view of Penygadair, the 2927-foot summit of Cadair Idris. This perch was the only bit of shade I could find that provided me with a view, but it was alarmingly steep, with a horrendous vertical drop on my right. After attaching myself to firm rock with a sling, I extracted my lunch from the rucksack. I removed my sketching gear, but unfortunately took my eyes off the lunch packet. Next thing I caught sight of my lunch disappearing over a 200-foot drop, and so had to make do with a banana and nuts.

My days on Cadair Idris always seem to have been blessed with glorious sunshine. One morning beside Llyn y Cau, early sunlight cast shadows across the shattered cliffs of Craig y Cau, towering above a mirror-smooth Llyn y Cau, which is said to be bottomless and of course harbours a monster. This is one of the wildest cwms in Wales, made famous by Richard Wilson's painting. As I sketched the scene a girl appeared and washed in the lake. I rubbed my eyes. Could she be a fairy? She walked along the shore to a partly hidden tent. No, fairies do not live in tents.

Unfortunately my days on the Carneddau range have not had such good weather. One January I camped beside Melynllyn, the Yellow Lake. All night hail and snow pattered on the tent skin. My lack of fitness after the Christmas break quickly became apparent the following morning on the climb up Foel Grach. When at last I reached the top I found no summit, just a flat plateau with mist merging into snow in a world of absolute white: no horizons, no corners, no little bits sticking up here and there. The wind quickly covered

Dolbadarn and Llanberis Pass

The castle is little more than a tower these days, but it is romantically situated at the entrance to the Llanberis Pass. Turner, in painting the scene, also wrote a poem about it.

Foel Grach Refuge Hut

most of my footprints with driven spindrift. I followed the compass needle along the ridge towards what I thought must be Foel Grach summit. Shortly afterwards I found the summit and gratefully tumbled into the refuge hut for a rest from the icy wind. Inside it was remarkably cosy and had been decorated with tinsel, streamers and balloons. There were even a Christmas card and a few twigs of holly. Later that morning I reached Carnedd Llewelyn, at 3484 feet the third highest peak in Wales. It was intensely cold and inhospitable so I did not hang around. However, by the time I had descended to Ffynnon Llugwy the landscape was bathed in sunshine. From here into the Ogwen Valley runs a tarmac road, a dreadful scar on the natural landscape. Many tracks are now being bulldozed across the mountains, apparently without any thought for what terrible eyesores they become.

Tryfan at Sunrise

This was the sight that greeted me one morning after a night camping beside Llyn Clyd on Y Garn. Mist boiled up out of Cwm Idwal to cause the summit of Tryfan to appear and disappear constantly.

A New Year's Day walk along the Nantlle Ridge gave me an uncomfortable battering from violent winds one time. The gusts threatened to toss me into Cwmfynnon from the exposed lip above the cliffs on the headwall. On Trum y Ddysgl I had to lean into an easterly wind which had already thrown me off my feet once. As far as the summit of Mynydd Drws-y-coed the route had been straightforward. On the far side towards Y Garn, however, is a steep ridge, a wilderness of rocks. Many of the rocks sloped awkwardly downwards, but worst of all they were coated with a veneer of ice. This made them ideal launching platforms to send the unwary shooting down the rock-strewn slope. Normally it would simply have been an interesting scramble, but today it needed great care; one slip could have been fatal. The position was complicated by the incessant wind which at times made me place a foot where I didn't want to – on ice – and over I went. Luckily my handholds held and soon I was sketching the ridge from relative safety.

Tryfan is everyone's favourite. Just over 3000 feet, it is one of the most popular climbs in the country. The classic route up Tryfan is the North Ridge, a fine airy scramble high above the Ogwen Valley. The most memorable of my several climbs here was on a March afternoon when a snowstorm swept across the valley. It was mesmeric, watching millions of flakes swirling down over a stygian Llyn Ogwen, gradually blotting out Penyrolewen. I crossed the head of a deep gully high up, to find the snowflakes on their way back up, blown by a strong wind. On reaching the summit I declined to make the traditional leap across Adam and Eve, the twin chunky boulders that stand on the highest point. In their icy state I would probably not have stopped before hitting Cwm Tryfan. Tryfan can be likened to a benign dragon. Once on the summit the logical extension is to follow the ridge south to Bwlch Tryfan, the dragon's neck. From here an exhilarating scramble leads up Bristly Ridge, the spiky combed head of the dragon, and one of the most popular scrambling routes. It should not be attempted by anyone without a head for heights.

The summit of Glyder Fach is a bewildering jumble of

Tryfan and Glyder Fach Panorama

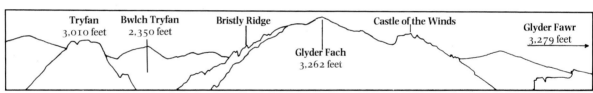

rocks that look as though some enraged giant has tried to rearrange the landscape. From here to the summit of Glyder Fawr is perhaps the wildest scenery in Britain. Halfway between the two summits stands Castell-y-Gwynt, Castle of the Winds, a spiked, bristling eminence, where

> Raw menace lurks in bladed air
> unsheathed to slice both rock and bone
> Of travellers who journey where
> the stricken crag defends its own
>
> JEAN M THOMAS

Glyder Fawr, at 3279 feet, is just seventeen feet higher than Glyder Fach. Its north face is shattered in a series of wild cwms, the most magnificent being Cwm Idwal. Thomas Pennant, the eighteenth-century Welsh naturalist, squire and traveller described the cwm as 'a fit place to inspire murderous thoughts'. It is at its most beautiful under snow and ice, the lake grey and icy, the Idwal Slabs, playground of climbers, decked in white strands of frozen rivulets, and the Devil's Kitchen a dark slit in the rocks above the head of Llyn Idwal, standing out against a wall of ice. When mist pours out of the Devil's Kitchen on a grim day it is easy to imagine the Devil at work within.

High above Cwm Idwal nestles Cwm Cneifion, a remote basin where, one February, I found the ice perfect for climbing. I began a long, steep gully climb which ended on the summit plateau of Glyder Fawr. Deep snow filled the gully in places, making climbing tedious, but progress was rapid where the grey-green ice cascaded over rocks in a thick

Adam and Eve

The twin summit boulders as seen from Cwm Tryfan: enlarged through binoculars.

Moelwyn Bach

mass. There is nothing more exhilarating to the ice-climber than to feel the ice-axe bite deep into solid ice.

Four times I visited the Moelwyns for a sketching trip. On the first three visits dense mist and heavy rain precluded much painting. The fourth trip, however, brought an improvement in the weather and after sketching the range from below I raced up Moelwyn Bach in an endeavour to beat the low cloud that hung over the hills. In my hurry I forgot to take ice-axe and crampons. Mist arrived to engulf the summit as I began my descent. I clambered down then found myself on awkward ice-glazed rocks. The best route, I reckoned, would be to descend a short gully that was filled with snow. Luckily my ice-hammer had been attached to the rucksack. I came to a stretch of ice. Slowly I descended backwards. With only one ice tool and my feet flailing about every time I tried a new foothold it became tragicomic. Light filtered through the mist, lighting up some rocks nearby. The temptation was too great, but how could I sketch in this position? I anchored the ice-hammer, put my wrist through the sling and held my sketchpad (which had been in my map case) in my left hand, whilst I drew with my right. One leg was in a semi-normal position, fairly secure on rock, but the other, held at an excruciating ninety degrees to the first, was totally insecure on a thimble of rock; at least it looked like rock. From this ungainly and hardly comfortable position I began sketching. I slipped twice, had to hold pencils and

Ice Gully, Cwm Cneifion
Seen dropping several hundred feet from near the top.

RIGHT:

Crib Goch from the head of the zig-zags

LEFT:

Cwm Cywarch

This is a delectable cwm in the Aran Mountains, the great crag in the background is Craig Cywarch. Every day I spent here on one trip was washed out, so much so that on the final night I had both feet wrapped in plastic bags, as the sleeping bag was saturated at the bottom.

brushes in my teeth, grazed a knee, lost a pencil and ended up with the most dreadful sketch.

Despite the vast number of visitors, and despite the erosion, Snowdon remains magnificent and unrivalled for rugged mountain grandeur. Its lines are graceful, its cwms and ridges sensational, and its call magnetic. It is arguably the most beautiful mountain in Britain. Yr Wyddfa, the proper name for Snowdon peak, is of course the highest summit in Wales. It is steeped in romance, with legends of giants, monsters and, naturally, King Arthur, whose last battle took place on Bwlch y Saethau, the Pass of the Arrows, below Snowdon summit. With his host he lies in a secret cave in the cliffs of Lliwedd, awaiting the call to come to the country's aid.

I first climbed Snowdon via the Pyg track on a cold January day when the clouds hung low. In those days the upper part of the zigzags was not so obvious, and I suddenly found myself on a sheer face with mist below me, and nothing else. Only when my companion enquired politely if I was happy with my route did I stop, for it was a sure sign that I was going the wrong way. We located the track and climbed steeply into the mist. The wind grew in ferocity to storm force, tossing us about like drunken skittles. We clung to the boulders to avoid being torn off the face. It was terrifying. I have never known such winds, and considered retreating. It was certainly the best idea, but with the wind

Yr Wyddfa (Snowdon) from Crib-y-ddysgl Ridge

from the rear it would have been highly dangerous to descend here. We could not see the main ridge above, but the safest plan seemed to be to climb to the ridge and descend by the Llanberis track. After many heart-stopping moments I forced my exhausted body over the snow cornice at the top and sat muttering with relief in the snow.

In later years I have tried to get up Snowdon when there is unlikely to be anybody else around. I had always wanted to be on the summit at sunrise, and so whilst camped below the intimidating cliffs of Clogwyn du'r Arddu I decided to race up to the summit next morning. I arose at 3.30am, ate breakfast in the dark and then climbed the Eastern Terrace, a weakness in the centre of the cliff. It makes a good scrambling route, as opposed to the extreme climbing routes on either side. 'Cloggy', as the cliff is affectionately called by climbers, is a Mecca for rock-climbers. The worst menace in the climb was not the gloom – for it was still dark– but stinging dust blown up by a light breeze. As I neared the top orange fingers cut across the sky above Y Garn. It lightened enough for me to take in the impressive rock scenery all around. Presently Y Garn was aflame in warm sunlight and I knew I had lost the race. A short plod over rough ground and I stood at the top of the zigzags above Cwm Dyli. Across the cwm, Crib Goch stood etched against an ice-blue sea of mist punctuated by peaks. I skulked beside a rock to shelter from the fresh wind, and sketched as two lads walked past. In my furtive pose I suppose they must have wondered what I was up to, and hurried past without speaking. I didn't linger as ice soon began to form on the watercolour.

My most exciting excursion on Snowdon was a winter traverse of the Snowdon Horseshoe. From Llyn Llydaw I climbed through mist, until at the Pyg track I found the clouds below me. Then came the scramble up Crib Goch's eastern ridge. Beneath, the mist rolled in waves of white foam, spilling over the twin peaks of Lliwedd like a giant saucepan boiling over. Moel Siabod floated like an island, five miles to the east. I sat on Crib Goch sketching the panorama of Horseshoe peaks, with Yr Wyddfa rising supreme in the centre. Quickly the crest began to get crowded, and it was time to move on. Halfway along the knife-edge ridge I stopped to draw, make notes and take photographs. This unfortunately meant being passed by several others, not an easy manoeuvre in such an exposed position, but it went by without incident. Down the pinnacles and up to Crib-y-ddysgl; all the while it was like being on the rim of a volcano with mist frothing up from the depths of Cwm Dyli. Once over Crib-y-ddysgl, however, cloud blotted out everything and the rest of the Horseshoe was done in dense mist. A poor ending to a glorious morning, but with hindsight that morning produced some of the best moments I've spent in the mountains.

Loch Lubnaig

9
MOONSHINE AND MIST
IN THE
SOUTHERN HIGHLANDS

From Loch Lomond to the southern edge of Rannoch Moor, the southern Highlands contain scenery of supreme beauty. Even when bad weather limits the views, the artist can be well rewarded for showing a little enterprise, for the lochs and glens are rich in subject matter. I spent several December days in poor conditions sketching at low level and amassing subjects whilst waiting for the peaks to clear. Loch Long, Loch Fyne, Loch Voil, Loch Katrine, Loch Lomond,

Loch Lubnaig and several others provided a wealth of material, but perhaps my favourite was Loch Ard, where mist floated just above the water to reveal the tops of pines and the distant snow-capped Ben Lomond. At 3192 feet, Ben Lomond is the most southerly of Scotland's 3000-foot mountains, or 'Munros'.

My first view of the Arrochar Alps was from the head of Glen Douglas, high above Loch Long. The Cobbler (Ben

The Cobbler from Glen Douglas

Ben Lomond and Loch Ard

Arthur) looked truly Alpine under snow. Although only 2891 feet high it is one of the most fascinating mountains in the Highlands, with an extremely striking profile of three peaks. It certainly made quite an impression on Turner as he did several studies of the mountain in 1801. I could hardly wait to climb the Cobbler, but had to sit patiently for clouds to pass in order to sketch it. When the work was complete I drove round the head of Loch Long and walked up beside the Buttermilk Burn. Above the trees the fierce wind bit into me. Soon I crossed the snow-line. My hopes of a close-up view of the Cobbler then faded into the rapidly descending mist. Then darkness. I stood alone with just the wind and snow flurries. With no further bidding I erected the tent in the lee of some large boulders. After a long drawn out meal I relaxed in candlelight. The wind increased, veering to the north east. The tent now became a sitting target, for the boulders no longer provided any shelter. A tremendous buffeting began to hammer the fabric, and at any moment I expected it to be hurled into the stream. Suddenly the candle blew out. It was fortuitous, however, as the bright moonlight revealed the fly-sheet in silhouette flying above the main tent and just about to depart from the remaining pegs. I pulled on my boots and raced outside into the howling wind, still in my underwear. A stunning sight gripped me. Above an ocean of mist Ben Lomond rose majestically, its snowy crown glistening in the moonlight. I forgot about the fly-sheet and my scantily clad body and, despite the cold, did a rapid sketch of the sublime scene. I could see for miles across mountain summits clad in snow, as though it were daytime. The cold tore into me. My hands began to go numb and my long-johns started to sparkle with frost-jewels. I threw the sketch inside the tent and secured the fly-sheet. The only rocks lay in the stream, so there was nothing for it but to jump in and haul several out to cover the tent pegs. Finally the ice-axe held the main guy-rope, and the tent was as secure as I could make it. Hot tea soon brought feeling back into my hands.

LEFT:
The Cobbler

Ben Lomond by Moonlight

A sketch done from the Buttermilk Burn on the Cobbler one beautiful, but cold, night.

The Cobbler, Centre Peak

This is the highest of the Cobbler's three summits, and on this occasion sported a chair, which I have included to give some idea of scale.

Thick mist frustrated views of the Cobbler and Ben Narnain next day, but hopefully I began the ascent at mid-morning. After a while I turned into the main corrie of the Cobbler, occasionally getting glimpses of a rocky peak through the fluctuating mist. Soon I was close enough to the south peak to sketch it, although much of it vanished from time to time. The cold, damp mist eventually persuaded me to put the drawing away. I crossed a field of boulders in deep snow. The incline increased to pretty steep snow below the south peak. The summit ridge was not visible as I kicked my way upwards. The going was easy, with deep, firm snow all the way to the ridge, where I found the wind fresher than ever. I climbed northwards along the ridge towards the centre peak, and scrambled over icy rocks to find specta-cular, if limited, views down steep gullies. The rocky buttresses were festooned with ice and cornices, a beauty in themselves. The silence of the mountain was broken only by the sighing of the wind round the rocks. In places, crevices gave notice that massive snow cornices were about to break off the ridge and plummet to unseen depths. Beauty and danger were very much close partners here.

The ridge led to the centre peak, the actual summit of the Cobbler. It stood about fifteen feet proud of the ridge, and comprised an uneven rectangular slab of rock with alarming drops on three sides. Perched on top, rather incongruously, stood an ordinary chair, though who would want to sit in such a precarious position was baffling. From the ridge I squeezed through a hole in the rock and found myself on a ledge on the western side. Beneath my narrow perch the rock fell vertically into the mist. Carefully I moved along the ledge, at all times keeping one foot jammed in a large crack. At the end came a scramble up slippery rock on to the final level, with abysmal drops all round. I sat on the summit rock for a few minutes before returning to my rucksack on the summit ridge.

I found the north peak less interesting. It is the easiest of the Cobbler's three peaks, though with a coating of ice it needed care. I then descended to the tent without attempting the south peak. The mountain was still shrouded in mist, but three days later I returned and managed to paint the Cobbler with cloud hovering a few feet above the summit. After finishing the work I decided to climb the mountain again, in the hope of getting some decent views. Alas, when I was less than a hundred feet from the col below the north peak, the mist returned and my hopes were dashed. I glissaded back down to the corrie.

Paradoxically, the best views I have experienced south of Crianlarich have all been at night during a full moon. By moonlight, even walking on rough terrain was no problem one night on the slopes of Cruachan, just north of Ben Lomond. So bright was the moon that I could see for miles. Ben Vane, Beinn Ime and Ben Vorlich across the far side of Loch Lomond gave unforgettable views. In some ways sketching by moonlight is simplified because much detail is lost, and it becomes more of a tonal study, where colours are less important.

On a cold February morning I left Bridge of Orchy, walking southwards along a track below the slopes of Beinn Dorain. The surrounding hills formed much of the subject matter for the poetry of Duncan Ban MacIntyre, 'Fair Duncan of the Songs', an eighteenth-century Gaelic poet who could not read or write. He memorized all his works and became one of the most renowned poets in the Highlands. Blizzards swept the landscape, but luckily the wind came from the north, so it was no problem. Each blizzard lasted about twenty minutes. I came across some Highland cattle beside a stream, and paused to sketch them in their miserable state. They were magnificent beasts, and despite their wild countenance seemed quite docile. I continued my way, following the line of the West Highland Way towards Tyndrum. From there I joined a track round the hillside to Cononish Farm, where I intended sketching Ben Lui, one of the most attractive peaks in the southern Highlands. As I contoured the hill I expected to see the mountain at any moment, so it was something of an anticlimax when I found not Ben Lui, but yet another raging blizzard sweeping down the glen towards me. Eventually it passed, leaving mist hanging in its wake. I carried on past the farm, hoping for a

Cononish Farm

Ben Oss came into view. But Ben Lui sulked in the gloom until another day.

Happily the following day dawned sunny and cold; ideal conditions to climb Ben Lui. Unfortunately it was a long walk in from Crianlarich, and with so many subjects to sketch it took ages. The clear air seemed to bring Ben More and Stob Binnein incredibly close, from down Strath Fillan. By mid-morning the lighting was perfect on Ben Lui when I began the sketch, the sun casting shadows across Central Gully and picking out the shape of the eastern face of the mountain, which rises to 3708 feet. When I crossed the stream at the foot of the mountain I was well behind schedule, and began climbing through deep soft snow. My aim was to climb Central Gully. The quality of the snow was far from perfect, but I made reasonable progress. At the foot of Central Gully I paused for a late lunch, and sat admiring the impressive complex of rocky architecture above me. Climbing and sketching do not always mix and now I found my work really holding me back. I continued the upward slog, trying to find the least deep snow and keeping rocks above me as far as possible to minimize any avalanche threat. The wind increased, blowing spindrift down my neck and over the camera, which quickly changed from black to white. It soon jammed and many potential photographs were lost. The angle grew steeper, the snow deeper and my stops for breath more frequent. Then snowflakes began to fall and the sunshine was obliterated. Without warning, the wind whipped into a frenzy, and I quickly found myself in a hostile, ferocious blizzard. One slip and I would shoot downwards hundreds of feet with little prospect of arresting a fall with the ice-axe in such soft snow. I traversed the slope towards the shelter of an overhang, axe in one hand and an ice-piton in the other. The landscape below had disappeared into a greyness alive with seething snowflakes.

Thankfully I reached the rocks and took stock of the situation. It was now late in the day and there was still quite a bit of climbing to do before reaching the summit. Navigation in the snowstorm was no problem here, but climbing would probably be hazardous, and at least part of

Highland Cow and Calf

On one occasion in the Highlands I came across a herd of Highland cattle in the middle of a road. As this was not particularly aesthetically pleasing I tried to encourage them into the river nearby so that I could do some sketching. However, they would have none of it, and after some time lowered their horns and scowled in such a way as to discourage further cajoling.

sighting of the mountain so that I could sketch it and so leave the next day free for climbing. However, as I ascended the track beyond Cononish Farm everything became extremely dark. Within minutes another blizzard was upon me, the most furious of the day. At this point I decided to return to the farm and at least get some work done there. Using watercolour to try and capture the mood of the storm, I sketched the farm, finding scant shelter in a dip in the ground. Here I skulked crablike, hoping no one was witnessing my antics. The blizzard slackened revealing trees bent before a strong wind. The western sky lightened and

Ben Lui

*This is one of the most shapely peaks in
the southern Highlands, particularly
when viewed from the Cononish River,
as seen here.*

Kilchurn Castle

This romantic ruin stands at the head of Loch Awe, at the foot of Ben Cruachan. It was built in the middle of the fifteenth century by Sir Colin Campbell, and became the home of the Campbells of Glenorchy.

From the collection of Alasdair White

Misty Morning, Glen Croe

the descent would have to be made in the dark. My camera was a block of ice, my hands virtually numb inside two pairs of gloves, and there was nothing visible, so sketching was pointless. I decided to turn back and try again tomorrow, but retreat was not easy. Poor visibility, aggravated by the wind blowing my cagoule upwards, hid my downward view, but after what seemed hours I was back at my lunchtime spot.

By the time I arrived at the foot of the mountain it was almost dark.

Sometimes it is harder, both physically and mentally, to retreat than to continue to the summit, but at least I knew I would some day return. I turned my back on the hills and hurried home through the gloaming.

Water of Nevis

10
DICING WITH THE DEVIL

Day broke frosty and clear, with mist dissolving higher up the glen. I left Glen Nevis Youth Hostel in warm sunshine, little realizing the epic that lay ahead. At Polldubh I left the road to ascend Sgurr a' Mhaim on the south side of the glen. The sunshine grew remarkably hot for a February morning and soon I climbed in shirtsleeves. To the right rose the shapely snow-bound peak of Stob Ban, whilst across the glen stood the lower buttresses of Ben Nevis. I paused many times to sketch and admire the view, more often as the slope became steeper. Eventually I found myself on a scree of white quartzite, awkward because it varied in size and stability, with patches of snow at intervals. The view of Ben Nevis was superb, and scenes of impressive mountain grandeur unfold-ed as I approached the summit ridge. Across a snow-field and I was soon standing on the 3601-foot summit of Sgurr a' Mhaim, the snow hard-packed with massive cornices. To the south lay a vast sea of peaks. Closest and most impressive of all was Stob Ban, from this angle an extremely beautiful sight. There was no sign of any form of civilization, only a landscape in its wild, natural form stretching as far as the eye could see. My route led southwards along the intimidating knife-edge Devil's Ridge switchback. It was already late as I began the descent from Sgurr a' Mhaim. By now I was tired after the effects of the climb with a full pack. From here onwards it was all snow and ice to Sgurr an Iubhair, over a mile away, with a thousand-foot drop on either side.

Ben Nevis from Sgurr a' Mhaim

RIGHT:
Stob Ban
A shapely peak in the Mamores, seen here from a snow-field high up on Sgurr a' Mhaim.

Progress became excruciatingly slow as I had no crampons. At times the ice-axe would bounce off the ice ineffectually and put my nerves to the test. It seemed so unreal being in such a highly dangerous, exposed position, yet lulled into dreamlike security by the warm sunshine.

At the highest point the snow came to a razor-sharp apex. I felt absolutely terrified and sure that I was about to die. Unlike climbing an ice gully there was nothing to hold onto, not even the questionable comfort of rocks on either side. My only contact with terra firma was the slippery wedge of snow that at any moment could send me hurtling downwards towards an abyss I could not see. Both hands were bleeding. My legs felt like lead. There are moments in the mountains when you push yourself beyond anything previously encountered. This was certainly one of those moments. Shadows lengthened. The peaks assumed a warm glow as the sun sank towards Loch Linnhe, just visible far beyond Stob Ban. Halfway along the ridge, without warn-

LEFT:
The Devil's Ridge

Mamores Sunset

This was the knife-edge ridge that gave me so many heart-stopping moments. On the left can be seen the summit plateau of Sgurr an Iubhair, over a mile away.

ing, the axe shaft caught in my camera case, wrenching it from the strap. I grabbed at it, slipped off balance and fell. My heart seemed to stop. The axe-pick bit deep into the snow, preventing a slide into oblivion, and I lay there gasping, almost screaming at myself in annoyance. Luckily the camera had caught in another strap. With one hand clinging to the axe I juggled with a clip to secure the camera. Both hands were so cold after being in contact with the snow that it was like trying to thread a needle with boxing gloves on. All the time I was aware of the appalling drops below.

Each step now was an intense experience, demanding absolute concentration. At last I reached the foot of the final slope leading to the flat summit of Sgurr an Iubhair. A steep slope with a black void below me. Just the place for an avalanche. The sun was setting as I crested the summit plateau, exhausted and mentally drained. The sunset over snow-clad peaks jolted me to do a sketch. There really didn't seem much point in rushing now, with 3300 feet to descend.

At first the descent went well, with just enough light from the glow in the western sky to make out the immediate area. Dramatic silhouettes of rocks pierced the glow. Somewhere in the darkness below lay Loch Leven. Beneath the snow-line I found myself stumbling down boulder-strewn slopes, steep and awkward. My torch was virtually useless, with only about five minutes left in the battery, so it could only be used in a dire emergency. I could hardly see anything, and moved forward deliberately, hoping there were no sudden vertical drops ahead. Eventually I found the old military road and trudged with greater confidence towards the lights of Kinlochleven, tired, but content with the day's events.

After a day of patching up wounds I left Kinlochleven in pouring rain, along the military road towards the head of Glencoe. One ankle was strapped up after straining it on the descent from the Devil's Ridge, but it held up well. This was desolate moorland, rimmed with snowy mountains, the rain turning to sleet as I gained altitude. Eventually I climbed over the pass and descended the Devil's Staircase into Glencoe. It must have been quite a feat to bring a coach and

Glencoe

RIGHT:
Allt Coire Mhorair

horses up the zigzags of the Staircase. Passengers had to get out and walk up, at times helping to push the coach. The route was also used by cattle drovers.

I turned into a grim, sullen Glencoe. It is hard to imagine a more fitting place for the macabre events of 13 February 1692 when soldiers under the command of Campbell of Glenlyon arose before dawn to kill their hosts, the Macdonalds. The troops fell upon the unsuspecting clansmen whilst they slept, killing men, women and children. Many escaped to the snow-covered slopes, only to die of exposure. Macaulay described the place as 'the very Valley of the Shadow of Death'. I walked down the glen, sketching here and there. Lower down I was overtaken by an enormous Scandinavian lass striding along with a rucksack twice the size of mine.

Yet another February I was on my way to Rannoch Moor. The mist thickened as the train climbed to the moor, where snow lay deep. It seemed strange to think that shortly

I would step out into that inhospitable white void and head off into the mist. At Corrour Halt the train stopped, and I jumped into a snowdrift. Somewhere underneath must have been a platform. I watched the red tail-light of the train vanish into the mist, and then found the track for Loch Ossian. It was not easy to follow the track, for in places the wind had blown snow across it, hiding any traces. The walk, however, was short and two sketches later I arrived on the shore. The combination of misty trees and frozen loch presented an interesting tonal study of varying shades of grey. The youth hostel had been abandoned for the winter months. Nothing stirred. After a while I left the loch to cross the moor to my next target, Loch Treig.

Out in the snowy waste of Rannoch Moor I could navigate only by compass. Visibility was strictly limited, so I had to place absolute faith in the instrument. The silence seemed unnerving. The ground rose and fell in waves of white, some of the snow deeply drifted. A herd of deer

Buachaille Etive Mor

This peak stands at the eastern entrance to Glencoe, and is seen here with the Kingshouse Hotel in the foreground.

appeared ahead, and momentarily glanced at me before dissolving once more into the whiteness. Here and there were deep pools of dark, still water, mirroring the banks of snow. This was quite a change from my previous visit to the moor, when I camped on a balmy September night with the moon silvering the waters of Loch Ba. At last the ground began to fall away and I picked up a distinct path. From there I made better progress down to Loch Treig. Although I carried a tent, my objective for the night was the bothy at Loch Chiarain. From Loch Treig I climbed up Glean Iola-irean, over rough ground covered in deep snow. It rapidly became purgatory. All afternoon I struggled on, getting increasingly tired with what seemed a never-ending slog. Each mile seemed like two. My lack of fitness began to tell, a common complaint on the first day of an expedition. The snow became softer and less predictable. I fell several times. Even when logic told me I was descending, that is, moving with the flow of the stream, my legs felt as though they were climbing. Where was Loch Chiarain? Eventually it came into view, but time still dragged by. Yes, there was a building, looking totally incongruous in such a wild setting.

In dismay I came to a stream swollen by the thaw. A snow-bridge crossed it, but would it hold? It did, and the way seemed clear for the final four hundred yards to the bothy. Here it was almost impossible to see where ground ended and loch started, for snow had drifted onto the frozen water. Another stream covered with snow barred my path. Half-way across, the inevitable happened: I crashed through the snow and into icy, black water. I fell forward, my rucksack flattening me face down. Searing stabs of pain shot up my right leg, seized by a severe attack of cramp as I lay jammed in the hole, treading water. Releasing the rucksack straps, I pulled myself onto firm ground and rolled over in the snow, massaging my leg. Gingerly I stood up and tested it. After initial protests it took my weight and once again I continued, prepared to erect the tent if things got too bad. Several times I fell before reaching the bothy, exhausted by weight, dis-tance, lack of fitness and that dreadfully soft snow.

The bothy was just a shell, with an upstairs and a

Meall na Cruaidhe

Snow bridges and drifts in a chasm on south-east flank

Waterfall above Loch Eilde Mòr

downstairs at one end. The floor was uneven, but it had a table, chairs and a sleeping platform. Candles and the stove soon made it cheerful.

I awoke late. A canopy of grey clouds precluded any sunshine, but at least it was dry with hardly any wind. I spent what was left of the morning in sketching around the bothy. After lunch I resumed my journey, heading initially towards the Blackwater Reservoir, beyond which lay a wall of impressive peaks. The snow was patchy, though deep in places, often causing detours to avoid awkward crevices. After a while I climbed higher in the general direction of Loch Eilde Mor, my next objective. I waded across streams, fell into streams through soft snow, and generally detested streams by the end of the day. At one stage I was almost completely covered in snow, and emerged with pockets full of the stuff. As time wore on it became evident that I would not see Loch Eilde Mor that day. More than ever, deep snow

Loch Eilde Mòr

hampered movement. Then I found my way completely blocked by a deep ravine. Huge, daunting crevices had formed on both sides where massive banks of snow had parted from the rocky sides. It looked a very hazardous river to cross, the water black and treacherous, fast-flowing and swollen. I sketched the problem as I pondered on a course of action, finally deciding to climb higher and cross at an easier point. Eventually I found a spot where there were no crevices; snow completely covered the river. Seeing no obvious fracturing, I carefully began to cross some thirty or so yards to a bank. The snow was firm, but I expected a sudden plunge into icy depths at any moment. Relieved, I reached the bank and moved forward with renewed energy. Half a mile further along the south flank of Meall na Cruaidhe I found a suitable but exposed campsite, not exactly flat, but close to a small brook. In the gloom I pitched the tent and settled in for the night, fully aware that I had barely covered more than one mile an hour all day.

It snowed softly during the night so that by morning the tent roof sagged alarmingly under the weight of accumulated snow. My boots were frozen solid and the tent pegs needed considerable effort to prise them out with an axe. I started late, but at this altitude the going was much easier on the frozen ground. Before long I dropped down to Loch Eilde Mor. The low temperature forced me on quickly. I walked round the western end of the loch where huge slabs of broken ice reared up in a weird pattern of jagged shapes. Along the military road I made excellent progress past Loch Eilde Beag, a veritable ice-rink. Then came the gradual climb up the pass towards Luibeilt, as light snow began to fall. At Luibeilt I met the fast-flowing Abhainn Rath, and after some time spotted an otter on the far bank. Every so often it would dive into the river, each time emerging with a small fish in its mouth. For about half an hour I watched and sketched as it fished and played, and climbed the steep bank to roll over on the grass, rubbing its back on the ground. Its exuberance was infectious, for I fairly bounced along after watching the little creature's antics.

For a while the walk upstream towards Glen Nevis was

Glen Nevis

Glen Nevis is one of the most beautiful and magnificent glens in Scotland. On the right the scene shows the Water of Nevis plunging through the gorge below Steall, whilst the scene on the left depicts the river further downstream. Finally the lower picture shows a scene near the head of the glen when the landscape is under deep snow.

amazingly beautiful world of plunging ice-forms, grey, green, blue and even white. Giant icicles dangle from crags, whilst

Quicksilver streams hang petrified
their stuttering escape denied
in rows of daggered ice
like teeth inside the mountain's jaw
await slow indolence of thaw
a pale sun might entice.

JEAN M THOMAS

Otter, Abhainn Rath

easy, over fairly flat ground. Where the river turned north one of its tributaries blocked my path. The bridge had been removed so, finding a suitable spot, I leapt across the stream, not quite reaching the far bank, and getting rather wet in the process. A few minutes later I caught sight of a new bridge that had been erected further upstream. Then came a marshy area, the watershed between the two glens, with great patches of thick ice. I crossed the infant Water of Nevis by a snow-bridge and headed down the glen. To my surprise shafts of sunlight began to break through the cloud layers, and Binnein Beag appeared to my left, with the sun hazily piercing the thin swirling mist. Peaks now began to appear all round as the mist lifted in places, and I actually found sketching pleasant and comfortable in the warm sunlight.

Rising above the north side of lower Glen Nevis is Ben Nevis, 4406 feet high, the highest mountain in Britain. From most angles it is a huge lump, but from the north east its secrets unfold. Here are the immense cliffs renowned to climbers, especially for their winter climbing. Its notoriety need not be repeated here, but once you have tasted the spectacular ice scenery of Ben Nevis, you are hooked. It is an

CIC Hut, Ben Nevis

I lunched beside the climbers' hut below the great north-east face of Ben Nevis, sharing my lunch with a collie called Nell, whose owner claimed that she could manage a grade 2 snow-climb without crampons. Just as well I suppose: it must be hard work fitting crampons on a dog. One of the climbers wore a bright yellow scarf turban-fashion with the ends flopping about like huge ears: a sort of Alpine goofy. Afterwards I sketched the hut from an extremely slippery position on an ice slope – almost a glacier – whilst anchored to an ice-axe. It was not dangerous, but certainly uncomfortable.

Loch Leven

Loch Pityoulish

II
THE ONE-HORNED
MONARCH OF
THE LAIRIG GHRU

The train pulled out of King's Cross and sped northwards into the February night. I sat feeling rather sick and more than a little apprehensive, eyeing the brand new ice-axe strapped to my rucksack with mixed feelings. This was my first winter mountain trip to Scotland, and rather ambitiously I had chosen the Cairngorms. The massive granite plateau of the Cairngorms rises to over 4000 feet in places, an exposed plateau often swept by snowstorms, driving, blinding, breath-snatching, with a ferocity and intense coldness that can quickly overcome lost or exhausted mountaineers. Much of the terrain is so devoid of features that navigation can be frighteningly difficult; a slight error fatal.

By morning tension built up further. The train battled uphill through an empty white landscape. Huge snowdrifts all but engulfed the railway line, and bodies of sheep lay frozen in the snow beside the track. I had picked a time when the snow lay exceptionally deep. To the east the Cairngorm range drew into sight, impressive yet menacing. I had decided to stay at Loch Morlich Youth Hostel this time, and found most of the residents were skiers. However, at dinner on the first night the chap on my right cheeringly announced that he had been buried in an avalanche the day before. Just the right conditions for avalanches, apparently, and Cairngorms' avalanches are pretty stunning.

Morning dawned fine, with cloud on the tops. I walked up the ski-road to Coire na Ciste. Nothing strenuous today, I told myself, just get used to the conditions. Above the ski-road conditions deteriorated. Strong headwinds tore sleet into my face and the deep snow made climbing very tiring and unpleasant. I turned back. At this time my sketching was limited in bad weather. I had to content myself with a few practice ice-axe arrests, flinging myself down gentle snow slopes – out of sight of skiers, of course – and getting extremely wet.

Back down in Glen More I headed up the Ryvoan Pass. This is an old robbers' route which cattle thieves used to escape from the Spey Valley. Halfway up the pass I came to Lochan Uaine, the Green Loch, said to be green because fairies washed their clothes in it. I sketched and grunted my way along the pass, and incredibly the day matured into evening. Sadly I had to turn back sooner than I normally would have done, as the western sky was now in its full glory: a sunset over the distant mountains, combined with threatening clouds and Caledonian pines carving black silhouettes in the foreground. Icy water rippled in the soft breeze, a series of cold greys gradually darkening as they sank deeper into the stream. So I had to be facing west to take advantage of this beauty, and common sense told me that it was hardly text-book mountaineering to walk backwards up the pass. Not much ground covered on my first day, but a lot of useful sketching done.

Dense mist greeted day two. Undeterred, I took the ski-bus to the lower chairlift station, only to find it clear, whilst below a white cloud enveloped Loch Morlich. I walked past the queues of skiers and started the climb up Cairngorm. I stopped to retie a bootlace. Suddenly I was almost pushed into a snowdrift as an over-enthusiastic reindeer nuzzled against my shoulder, at the same time eyeing my rucksack with its doleful eyes. Good job it didn't have any horns! These ex-Lapland reindeer were introduced to the Cairngorms in the early fifties, and seem to thrive there.

Mist closed in. Gone were the skiers. I followed the ski-tow pylons upwards, then heard a muffled noise. Could it be an avalanche? I strained to listen. Yes, it was approaching from above. Desperately I tried to recall whether any of the mountaineering text books recommended hiding behind ski-tow pylons in the event of an avalanche. How should I hold the ice-axe? By now I was convinced a bone-crushing avalanche was about to come crashing out of the mist. Directly above me a line of skiers slowly came into view, shuffling towards me tentatively, arm in arm as though doing a conga in diving boots.

Above the top station I climbed into a total whiteout, something I had never experienced before. The distance to

RIGHT:
Ryvoan Pass at Sunset

David Bellamy

Cairn and Spindrift on Cairngorm

A wild and inhospitable place at the best of times, the summit plateau of Cairngorm is a veritable white hell in a blizzard or windswept spindrift.

the summit was not great and I had calculated the alteration of compass-bearings in advance. However, the absolute whiteness was bewildering and disorientating. Which was up and which was down? At times I fell over because the ground was further away than I thought; at others my foot hit the ground where I didn't realize there was any, and so over I went again. The wind grew stronger, obliterating the footprints. I was only a few hundred yards from the upper station, yet I felt alone and completely reliant on my sense of navigation.

A cairn appeared out of the mist, covered in frozen spicula, a post protruding from its centre flagged with ice. Dare I stop and sketch it? I feared I might lose my sense of direction and quickly get chilled, but carried out a rapid sketch. After a few minutes I began to feel the cold and hastily stuffed my art gear into the rucksack. As I continued the climb, the ground levelled off gradually. Suddenly I stopped in my tracks. My hair stood on end. Out of the mist appeared a huge animal, the size of a donkey, the shape of a wolf. I gripped the ice-axe, prepared to defend myself against this massive creature. Then it vanished as suddenly as it had appeared, but I remained uneasy. Crossing to where it had stood I found its footprints almost as big as my own.

Presently I found the summit but did not stay long, eager to get away from the constant battering of spindrift and the thought that the beast was 'lurking out there somewhere'. Descent, however, was not so easy. Gone were the footprints, and several times I felt myself sliding off course, but before long the upper station loomed up out of the gloom. I later found out that one of the lads who serviced the meteorological station on Cairngorm owned an Alsatian, which must have been my beast. Without any feature to compare it with, the animal had appeared gigantic. The natural tendency in whiteouts is to believe that objects are far larger than they actually are.

My next excursion involved a walk to the Lairig Ghru Pass. Initially my path threaded through Glen More Forest, part of an old natural pine forest, where the sun shone through the pines, turning it into an enchanting place. The pristine snow sparkled, and here and there I came across pleasant snowy glades. Out of the forest the ground steepened and progress became snail-like. The sun grew hotter and I sweltered in shirtsleeves, at times waist-deep in snow. Half a mile took over an hour to cover, but higher up the hard-packed snow allowed more reasonable speed to be attained on my way towards the Chalamain Gap. At times, when crossing the snow, running water could be clearly heard beneath me, and I imagined all sorts of horrific dangers. I expected at any time to plunge through a crust of snow into a stream fifty feet below.

I crested a ridge and stopped in my tracks. There was the Lairig Ghru, an immense slit in a vast mountain wilderness of snowy slopes. A desolate prospect, with Brieriach rising into the clouds. A reindeer stood nearby, and as I drew nearer I could see it only had one horn. What a sad-looking beast; hardly the monarch of the glen. It cantered towards me, crashing through the snow like an ungainly hippo dancing in mud. Further down I found more reindeer, and for a while we danced round in circles as I tried to line one up for a photograph with the Lairig Ghru as a backdrop. It must have seemed quite a bizarre ritual to anyone watching, and although at the time I was unaware of anyone around, the resulting photographs did reveal two distant figures. Soon I was surrounded by reindeer, all so affectionate and eager to eat my map.

Loch Avon

I descended into the pass, dwarfed by the amazing scale of the scene, and carried out a number of sketches. Clouds hid the upper reaches of Ben Macdui on the eastern side of the pass. At 4296 feet it is the highest point in the Cairngorms and the second highest mountain in Scotland. The slopes of the mountain are said to be haunted by Fear Liath Mor, the Big Grey Man, who has chased people, taking one step to every four or five of theirs.

> There Fear Liath Mor – the big grey man –
> leaves giant footprints where
> shapeless shadows skulk in mist
> and only reindeer dare.

JEAN M THOMAS

Loch Avon, in the heart of the Cairngorms, has a profoundly remote feeling about it. At the head of the loch the wildness is striking, the scene dominated by the Shelter Crag below which lies a confusion of boulders. Amidst this rocky debris stands the Shelter Stone, a rock as large as a cottage. It is an ideal shelter, with a low entrance in one corner through which it is easy to crawl into the pitch darkness. My torch picked out the visitor's book, a tatty affair retaining only one completed page. According to the various guides the stone can accommodate up to six climbers, eighteen armed cut-throats, eight sheep with sixteen shepherds, or ... The list is endless.

Most of my exploits in the Cairngorms have been dogged by bad weather. One advantage of this has been that I am more or less forced to seek low-level subjects unless I'm up high when the clouds descend. One such time was when I left Linn of Dee to find Corrour bothy at the lower end of the Lairig Ghru. It was more of a challenge walk than a sketching trip, as I had precious little daylight left when I set

Lairig Ghru with Reindeer

Here the Lairig Ghru presents a savage background on a day of sunshine. The reindeer were quite friendly and obviously used to contact with humans.

The sheer scale of these mountains is awesome, with mountains on both sides of this pass reaching to well over 4200 feet. Collection of Mrs AJ Bellamy

Shelter Stone

The shelter stone is a haven in an absolute wilderness, affording protection from the elements. Inside it is dark but cosy, with hardly a draught.

out on a late autumn afternoon. This was a sixteen-mile round trip: a real 120-paces-to-the-minute task.

With the wind and drizzle in my face I began at a fine pace along the tarmac road across the estate to Derry Lodge. Low clouds draped drearily over the peaks but I sensed more excitement awaited me further up the glen. At the lodge the road ended, but a track continued up Glen Luibeg. The scenery grew wilder, with Caledonian pines framing a background of misty mountains. The river rapidly became swollen, the rain heavier. I sketched the scene, then charged on at twice the speed to make up lost time. Luibeg Bridge, happily perched on rocks well above a clawing torrent, provided yet another sketch. Then the going became more exposed to the elements, the path rougher and my legs more tired. More sketches. This was ridiculous, I thought, fuelling myself with chocolate and breaking into a powerful rendering of 'Calon Lan' to keep spirits high. I had been in the hills over ten days, so I was almost at peak fitness. The challenge

and scenery fired me with uncommonly high morale. How much further? No sign of the Lairig Ghru. I began to flag, realizing that despite my excellent pace I was falling behind time. To continue would mean that much of the return journey would be in the dark. Still, I must be pretty close now. I forced myself on, watching for a hint of the Devil's Point, a peak which dominated the bothy, but ahead just mist and rain, with gentle curves of rising slopes.

Almost on the point of giving up I caught sight of the pass, with the Devil's Point emerging from the clouds. A few minutes later I spotted the bothy, a tiny haven amidst a giant wilderness. I gradually worked my way down into the Lairig Ghru, which climbed into the clouds in the distance. The bothy lay on the far side of the raging River Dee. A fairly new bridge spanned the torrent, but its approaches on either side were awash. I charged across a cloying sea of mud and reached the bridge, realizing immediately that I could get across, but if the river was rising rapidly would my retreat be

Luibeg Burn

Luibeg Bridge

OPPOSITE:
Loch an Eilean
*A delightful loch surrounded by pine
woods. The castle was used in 1715 to
imprison a local on suspicion of having a
desire to join the Hanoverian cause.*

cut off? This was no time for fine calculations. I raced across and jumped onto firm ground on the far side, before running up to the bothy. My sketches were carried out with the minimum of fuss, capturing a number of angles before making an entry in the bothy log book. As I retraced my steps to the bridge, evening was closing in. Water lapped over the bridge supports as it swirled in eddies beyond the torrent, but I managed to leap on and cross without mishap. It's easy to see how bridges get washed away in the Highlands. I shuddered as I looked back at the raging waters.

At first the return journey proved easy. I had rested, the wind was behind me, and I had to be single-minded about

getting back to the Linn of Dee. I climbed out of the pass and glanced back at the wild scene, pausing for a moment to reflect on how lucky I was to be able to witness such rugged grandeur. Perhaps if I reached the car all right I could feel justified in having won the challenge, but one can never 'beat' the mountain. It's not a game of winners and losers. Mountains in this wild state reduce one to utter humbleness even when leaving them triumphantly. However, there were still many miles to cover, and the hills probably had one or two tricks up their sleeves. As often happens, the wind turned as I started the descent into Glen Luibeg, and once again I faced strong headwinds. By now I was exhausted, but

Main Cairngorm Ridge from
Loch Morlich

*On the left is Cairngorm, in the centre is
Coire an t' Sneachda and on the right is
Coire an Lochain.*

LEFT:
Corrour Bothy

The bothy is a sturdy building standing on a grassy verge above the River Dee. In the background is the Devil's Point. Its enormous boiler-plate slabs were glistening in the rain, but I did not tarry long to put too much detail in the sketch, as the river was rising and I feared being cut off.

spurred on by the oncoming darkness. By the time I arrived at Derry Burn it was completely dark, and as usual my torch was fit only for the occasional flash. Once on the tarmac road, however, the going was straightforward.

The Cairngorms are a fascinating playground, tough and demanding, claiming many lives. They are constantly under threat of development in the form of long ugly tracks being bulldozed across the mountainsides, and extensions to the skiing areas. Neither of these aspects enhances the natural beauty, and positively detract from their wild grandeur. These hills do not deserve such vandalism.

Evening Light, Western Highlands

12
THE WILD AND WET WEST

Perhaps more than any other part of mainland Scotland the western Highlands appeal to the romantic. Castles such as Eilean Donan and Tioram are sited in beautiful locations on the edges of lochs; the hills are steeped in historical associations of the 1745 rising, and there are often glorious sunsets over the sea lochs, many of which run deep into the mountains. This was where the Jacobite standard was raised in 1745. The hills are a fitting backdrop to the flight of Bonnie Prince Charlie following the battle of Culloden, and there are several caves where the prince is said to have hidden during the pursuit. Though romanticized, the aura of the daring adventure cannot escape those who set foot in these hills. It must have been a desperate struggle being a fugitive for months in such inhospitable mountains.

Naturally, this is the wettest part of Scotland. All my visits have been to the accompaniment of heavy rain. After the first few days of listening to rain pattering on canvas, and when everything I touch is soaking, the snug feeling wears off. Rivers can quickly become impassable, and then the guessing game of 'will there be a bridge?' begins. Not all bridges are marked on the map. Not all bridges that are marked are still there. Anyway the place would lose its remoteness if every river had a bridge; much fun would be lost.

Shelley might well have had the western Highlands in mind when he wrote:

– the hill
Looks hoary through the white electric rain,
And from the glens beyond, in sullen strain
The interrupted thunder howls; above

Castle Tioram, Loch Moidart

Old Bridge, Loch Cluanie

One chasm of heaven smiles, like the age of love
On the unquiet world

These mountains are among the roughest. Walkers and climbers are few and far between, and soon lose themselves in the vast spaces. On an early visit I chose one of the wettest autumns on record and whilst camping near Loch Ailort experienced continuous rain each day. I sketched the loch with rain and mist constantly changing the view, and lighting falling in a concentrated spot as though orchestrated by a Rembrandt brush-stroke. At Loch nan Uamh I stood beside the loch, transfixed by intense light falling on dark waters as again rain and mist veiled the mountains, creating an air of mystery. This was the scene of departure of Prince Charlie as he boarded a French frigate at anchor in the loch in September 1746. A cairn marks the spot where he left Scotland. Nearby, a rowing boat bobbed up and down, and it took little to imagine the prince's headlong flight as he was rowed to the ship.

Further south I came to Loch Moidart, on a gloomy September evening. I took out my wet tent and it became even wetter. Water had seeped into the plastic envelope containing my large sketchbook so that the pages were stuck together, forming beautiful circular blobs on my sketches. Rain had also penetrated inside my rucksack pockets, one of which was covered in bright red and yellow paint from the palette. My brush case had been inserted upside-down, and so all the wet brushes had a peculiar ninety-degree twist, making it hard to paint. I retired to my sleeping bag in disgust.

On the following day I was startled to find that the rain had stopped, making sketching a comparatively simple task. Loch Moidart is beautifully surrounded by wooded hills, with Castle Tioram, once the home of Macdonald of Clanranald, sited picturesquely on a rock by the shore.

One wet September morning I left the hamlet of Morvich at the northern end of the Five Sisters of Kintail and walked up Gleann Lichd. My objective was the youth hostel at Alltbeithe, some twelve miles distant. The sides of the glen rose steeply, with Beinn Fhada on my left and the Five Sisters to the right. Low cloud restricted views of the peaks, and rain dampened enthusiasm for sketching. At that time I had not developed wet-weather working to any great degree.

At first it was a gentle climb beside the River Croe, along what must be a pleasant stroll on a warm summer's day. Above Glenlicht House I crossed two bridges, the second of which was suspended high above the Allt Grannda by wires. Not only did it slope alarmingly to one side, but it seemed ready to collapse at any moment. Gingerly I stepped onto the wet, sloping planks, trying to ignore the frothing, churning water below. Surely this structure could not hold up much longer. I fairy-footed across and with relief set foot on the opposite bank. Still, it made an interesting subject. From here the route became more rugged as the gradient steepened. The mountainsides closed in and the river was forced through a gorge, tumbling down a series of waterfalls. These did not make convenient subjects as it was difficult to obtain a reasonable viewpoint from such a high angle. Drizzle fell all afternoon, and eventually I came to the head of the glen and began to descend towards Glen Affric. The path passed the ruin of Camban, after which the youth hostel soon came into view. The path swung down to the River Affric and I had to cross a tributary. There was no bridge but the water was not too deep. At the end of a day when already soaking wet it hardly seems to matter about wetting the feet a little more.

I strode up to the hostel, a large hut in the middle of a wide strath. The door suddenly burst open, a figure leapt out and ran excitedly to greet me. The warden was obviously glad of custom after six months in his lonely retreat. Thankfully he had ample room and it was gratifying to change into dry clothes and sup warm tea. Later, after supper, we all sat round a log fire, illuminated by a paraffin lamp. Shadows cast by the fire flickered up the walls, whilst boots and an odd

Loch Shiel

This small loch nestles below the Five Sisters of Kintail. It was near here that in 1719 a contingent of Spanish troops landed in Kintail to assist Jacobite forces. They were routed by government troops further up the glen.

assortment of clothes dried near the fire. A Norwegian couple, the warden and three Scots lads crammed into the room. The cosy, friendly atmosphere was typical of the more remote, simple youth hostels. There were no televisions; no games machines; no running water; no electricity. For someone used to spending night after night in a lonely tent it was an opportunity to exchange experiences with fellow walkers.

Morning brought an improvement in the weather: it was still cloudy, but dry. Washing arrangements at the hostel were provided by a small burn that ran past the building. A trough had been erected to give a constant cascade. The wash invigorated me. The hostel is well sited at the junction of routes converging from several directions. It stands in a valley ringed by mountains, having an air of peaceful remoteness. Time seemed to stand still here and I felt sad to have to leave the place.

I trudged due west, following a footpath up Gleann

Wire Bridge over the Allt Grannda

Gniomhaidh, this time with Beinn Fhada to the south, before climbing up over Bealach an Sgairne. Through the gap a steep descent led past waterfalls. Slowly the mountains opened out until I reached Strath Croe and finally back to Morvich. Despite a shortage of sketches the trip had been interesting; my first walk of any distance in Scotland.

Since then, sketching techniques have improved, so I was better prepared on a later expedition to Knoydart. On the first morning sun began to filter through dark clouds, sending patches of light across the rugged slopes on the north side of Glen Dessary. The morning was fresh and my journey through the hills to Loch Nevis proved uneventful. As I dropped down to the loch the scenery became more dramatic. The forlorn and roofless ruin of Finiskaig provided an interesting subject with Loch Nevis in the background, cradled in the hills. Down at the shoreline I sketched Sourlies bothy from a number of angles. The solid stone building was opened as a bothy in 1977 and is well used, according to the log book. I carried on along the shore. Across the head of the loch the mountains fell steeply into the water, their upper parts wreathed in mist, dramatic and ethereal. Producing my sketchbook was a signal for rain to start falling, but it was only light. I painted a glorious ethereal mess, and laid it on the ground whilst I heaved on my rucksack once more. Alas, I had not closed the top flap. A food bag fell out, directly onto the wet sketch, covering it with muesli and butter, hence improving the work considerably. The weather closed in and I was then glad to get the tent up.

Swirling clouds and light rain greeted me when I flung the tent-flap back at daylight. As I began working on my first sketch three stalkers arrived and chatted awhile. All three were nattily dressed in deerstalkers and tweeds. During the deerstalking season tensions often mount between walkers and stalkers. It is easy to see how the latter become enraged when brightly clad walkers frighten away deer after the best part of a day has been spent manoeuvring into position. For

The Saddle

A view from the north-east ridge of Sgurr nan Eugallt one evening.

my part, I'm not too keen to be on the wrong end of a high-powered rifle, apart from other considerations. Happily, I've always found estates very courteous and helpful when making enquiries.

My path traced the west bank of the River Carnach upstream into truly remote terrain. It rained all the way, which usually speeds my progress, but I could not pass through such a glorious landscape without doing several sketches. At one point the clouds parted for a brief moment, to expose Luinne Bheinn towering high above the glen, an opportunity too good to miss. Then the mountains closed in, the river tumbling through a wooded defile. White, foaming water cascaded between dark grey rocks. The whole mountainside seemed awash. Trickles became streams. For a while the path was a switchback of climbs and descents, then suddenly at the head of the gorge it opened out dramatically. The trees stopped. The river flowed dark and slow moving beneath vertical, black cliffs festooned with lush vegetation. Rain still hammered down, but through the moving veil I could make out peaks and slopes beyond the dark cliffs. This was the north-west buttress of Ben Aden, a spectacular scene, straight out of Tolkien, but extremely difficult to capture on paper in such a torrential downpour. Attempting to tuck the wet sketch into the map case was like trying to thread a live eel through a keyhole. The route turned north-eastwards, climbed a little further and then opened out onto an uncomfortable wide boggy stretch. Where the Carnach made a sharp turn towards Lochan nam Breac we parted

Loch Arkaig

In the foreground are the ruins of an old patrol post used by Hanoverian troops during the '45 rebellion to keep the glen under surveillance. It would have been manned during Prince Charlie's flight from Culloden, after which he passed this way in making his escape.

David Bellamy

Loch Nevis and Sourlies Bothy
Collection of the author

River Carnach and Cliffs

Here at the north-west foot of Ben Aden the River Carnach bends round steep, dark cliffs.

River Carnach

Deerstalking

Deer are still brought down off the hills by horse, although apparently Arabs have been known to use helicopters. Many of the weaker deer die during the savage winters in the Highlands, and it is the weaker stags that are culled during the deerstalking season.

company and I climbed steeply north-westwards. I paused frequently to recover breath. A movement in the sky caught my attention, and two eagles soared over the crags above. Soon I picked up the path which rose to the col below the east ridge of Luinne Bheinn, and descended into Gleann Unndalain. The rain persisted and crossing the Allt Gleann Unndalain necessitated wading through deep fast-flowing water.

Barrisdale came into sight, with Loch Hourn in the distance, for all the world like a Chinese watercolour through a film of falling rain. Did a bridge still exist down there? Gratefully I found one after a long descent, and then quickly reached the bothy. It made a spartan but dry home for a few nights. The log book showed that the place had constant use during the summer months, full of people who seemed to want to get away from other people. Weather and midges had several mentions.

Ladhar Beinn, one of the jewels of Knoydart, looked uninviting from the lower end of Coire Dhorrcail. Thick mist covered the top, whilst the magnificent cliffs at the corrie

Ben Aden and Loch Quoich

head-wall stood out dark and sombre. I crossed the stream and climbed a steep slope to the end of the ridge of Druim a' Choire Odhair. Although it was only September the conditions were icy on top. Not far along the rising ridge I climbed into dense mist, disturbing a ptarmigan. The ridge narrowed to a knife-edge, and undulated sharply. Not a particularly healthy spot in such a cruel wind. I came to a T-junction of ridges, and turned right for the summit, which I reached by early afternoon. Then I retraced my steps to the junction. I was descending at last, along the rim of the cliffs at the head of Coire Dhorrcail, disturbing two more ptarmigan on the way. The suddenness with which they take off is startling. Below the cloud level I could see Loch Hourn a long way down. Eventually I dropped down into the vast corrie and returned to Barrisdale, rather disappointed with the days' events.

The final leg of this long circuitous expedition was to return to Glen Dessary via Loch Quoich. I reached the loch after walking down Gleann Cosaidh, and then followed the shoreline in a south-westerly direction towards Sgurr na Ciche. The shoreline fascinated me. Marbled rocks, flecked with a variety of colours, rose out of the water, at times in strange formations. Some were pure white, some candy-striped and some glinted with metallic spots. The rocks gave way in places to peat hags and the remains of an old Caledonian forest. Twisted roots and sculptured patterns of red wood had been laid bare by eroded peat. The wood was firm, the shapes like a form of abstract art. From this amazing foreground the eye travelled across the loch, which was whipped into small waves by a fresh breeze, then to the distinctive summit of Sgurr na Ciche. Progress round the loch was hampered by my inquisitiveness. I then caught sight of the rugged profile of Ben Aden rising to the right of Sgurr na Ciche, shafts of light falling down its northern flanks from an angry sky. At the head of Loch Quoich frogs leapt in profusion, as though eager to trip me up. One even jumped onto my boot. After this came a real slog: up the north-east corrie to the summit of Sgurr na Ciche. This proved to be quite a battle, but the view from the summit was ample reward, with mountains stretching in all directions. One view can be worth ten thousand steps.

Croft at Luib

Collection of Mrs C A Bellamy

13
SCRAMBLES ON SKYE

For the artist, Skye is a land of incredible contrasts. On the one hand there are gentle landscapes sprinkled with crofts, and on the other there is the stark drama of the Black Cuillin and the crazy rock formations of the Trotternish. Additionally the island is steeped in romantic legend, and evokes a powerful impression on the emotions, artist or not. Here the weather is at its most fickle, changing with remarkable suddenness. Rain, wind and mist were the order of the day when I climbed up to the Old Man of Storr, a leaning basalt pinnacle on the Trotternish ridge north of Portree. The rock shapes are fantastic and when mist is swirling round them they assume even weirder proportions. At times mist can help the artist by flowing between rocks, crags and pin-nacles, thereby outlining the feature that would otherwise be lost against a background of rock face. This place would be a fitting retreat for a coven of witches, its sharp, angular rock-forms giving an eerie backdrop. The crowning glory is the Old Man himself, standing 160 feet high, a prominent landmark for miles.

I journeyed north to the Quiraing, a name said to derive from a Gaelic word meaning pillared stronghold. I approached the enormous amphitheatre, formed amidst rocky walls below a sheer cliff face. So fierce was the wind that waterfalls were unable to fall over the cliffs, being driven upwards to disperse in droplets. The final climb up to the Needle, a crazy pinnacle over 100 feet high, was quite a trial.

Strange rocks of the Storr —

The Old Man of Storr →
160 feet high

?
Rock with windows

The Sanctuary →

Rocks of the Storr

The Needle, Quiraing

The figure climbing just above the foot of the Needle gives some idea of scale.

Not content with the most fearsome wind, the elements lashed stinging rain into my face. On reaching the foot of the Needle, however, strong sunshine filled the hollow. I ascended a huge cleft in the cliffs above the Needle to sketch it from the most dramatic angle. Unfortunately I chose the most windy position, where furious blasts funnelled their way through the gap. The wind rocked me violently even though I hugged the cliff, at times spinning me round and threatening to toss me down the steep slope. It was extremely laborious carrying out the watercolour. Everything had to be done slowly and deliberately so as not to drop brushes, pencils or palette down the slope or have the sketch torn away. I needed at least three hands, but in the end managed a passable attempt, considering the handicaps.

After further sketches of some of the most amazing rock scenery in the British Isles, I retreated to explore the crofts of the Trotternish. There are still some superb examples of old thatched crofts on Skye, and it is heartening to see that many are being renovated and used, mainly as tourist attractions. As with all such buildings, my artistic preferences are biased towards the ruinous old crofts, their stones green with moss, weeds sprouting from decaying thatch, and surrounded by tumbledown, overgrown outbuildings and drystone walls. The crofts on Kilmuir are especially fine examples, and stand close to the graveyard where Flora Macdonald is buried. It was here that Flora landed with the Young Pretender in 1746 when he was being pursued by Cumberland's troops.

Of course, the biggest attraction to the mountaineer on

Croft

Sgurr Alasdair from the Glen Brittle Track

Sgurr Dearg		Sgurr Alasdair	Sgurr Sgumain
3,209 feet		3,257 feet	3,108 feet
	Sgurr Mhic Choinnich		
	3,111 feet		

Great Stone Shoot

Skye is the Black Cuillin range. These hills are very different from anything on mainland Britain. They seem to change colour more violently than elsewhere: black and forbidding when under lowered cloud, they can be quickly transformed by the sun into pink or ochre; against evening light they can be fiery red. Their sharp, dramatic outline cuts deep contrasts between sky and rock, sunshine and shadow, the black gabbro rock sombre and unyielding. They are not mountains to be trifled with, and make the foolhardy pay dearly for any mistakes.

One sunny day I left the Glen Brittle campsite and followed the well-worn track to Coire Lagan. The great cirque of jagged cliffs towered impressively above. My route was up the Alasdair Stone Shoot, a 1200-foot scree slope which falls from a col just below the summit of Sgurr Alasdair. The toil upwards was relentless, accompanied by much sliding, but in time I gained the col where a great blast of wind greeted me. The scramble to the summit was short, but made hazardous by fierce gusts of wind. Alasdair, at 3257 feet, is the reigning peak of the Cuillin. Below the summit I sat down between two rocks to admire the view out to sea, with Rhum and Eigg floating in a thin haze. Strong gusts blew into my face and the sunshine lulled me into a false sense of security. I relaxed and for a few moments daydreamed. Without warning I found myself falling. The wind had taken a sharp reverse, caught me unawares and I fell towards a horrific drop, unable to stop myself. Amazingly, I jerked to a halt as suddenly as I had started. My rucksack frame had snagged in rocks and held me whilst I scrambled to safety. It had been a lucky escape. I returned to the col after taking in the Cuillin Ridge, and then shot down the scree in a rapid exhilarating descent. Within very few minutes I once again stood beside the lochan in Coire Lagan.

Late one September I left the Sligachan Hotel heavily laden with tent and supplies for several days. I aimed to cross over the main ridge to Loch Coruisk via Coire na Creiche, and climb parts of the ridge. This, however, was going to be one trip that didn't end up quite the way it was planned.

Sketching as usual slowed me down considerably. As I skirted the lower slopes of Bruach na Frithe and into Coire na Creiche I came into the full force of the wind, charged now with steady rain. Gradually the clouds lowered. The mountains turned black and forbidding. I crossed a series of streams, then turned up Coir' a' Mhadaidh. The rain now lashed down, accompanied by thick mist. Ahead my path seemed to be blocked by sheer cliffs of dark-grey gabbro. It was senseless to continue, but if I could get down to Loch Coruisk tonight, who knows what tomorrow might bring? I sketched the cliffs in watercolour. It seemed a ludicrous composition. Three times the colour was washed off the

Cuillin Ridge
This is a view from the col at the head of the Great Stone Shoot on Sgurr Alasdair, seen in evening sunlight. Towards the left of the picture, on the ridge, can be seen the Inaccessible Pinnacle, one of the few summits in Scotland that calls for rock-climbing to reach the top.

Coir a' Mhaidaidh
The massive cliffs that blocked my path.

Pinnacle Ridge, Sgurr nan Gillean

paper, but the final application stuck, even though it formed crazy blots when pressed inside the map case.

A few verses of 'Cwm Rhondda' restored confidence when I resumed the march towards the seemingly impregnable cliffs, assuring myself that there must be a route up to the left. The going underfoot was rocky. At the foot of the cliffs I crossed a stream tumbling through rocks and, sure enough, found my way up a scree gully to the left. The scree was exasperatingly steep and the top was not visible. I began ascending the unstable scree with renewed determination. The light by this time had grown extremely poor. The weight of my enormous wet rucksack began to take its toll and the number of steps between each rest became fewer. After what must have been about half an hour the gully still climbed interminably above, steepening, with water cascading off every rock. I began to think about a campsite, as dusk was now gathering. There was no likelihood of a reasonable site until I'd dropped down some way on the Coruisk side. I became so engrossed in the thought of getting a site that my concentration began to waver. The gully opened out to a wide fork on the right, with a wide sloping shelf. I paused, but decided to carry on straight ahead. The route increased in difficulty. Soon I found myself climbing small waterfalls. Rocks that would have provided an enjoyable scramble when dry became targets of verbal abuse in the downpour. Each hold produced a trickle of water down my arm. It certainly dampens all desire for artistic expression when there is a steady flow of rainwater through your armpit.

Eventually I saw what appeared to be the top: a gap in the rocks above. Even that took some considerable effort. I rested on the crest of the ridge, able to see little in the misty semi-darkness. Only rocks, slabs and crags, a truly savage place. It was vital that I should get down to a site as quickly as possible, so I squelched noisily down the rocky slopes. Ahead the prospect appeared forbidding: out of the mist loomed vast black shapes punctuated by the stark whiteness of foaming, falling water. I followed a stream downwards, hopping, scrambling and jogging, a speed born of desperation. The Cuillin, when angry, is no place to hang around.

I found myself in a hanging cwm. It was dark. I stopped and took stock of my surroundings. All around the sound of cascading water grew more threatening; here and there were patches of grass. I descended further and found route-finding a nightmare. Suddenly the stream plunged over the edge of huge black precipitous rocks, into an impenetrable darkness. It was suicidal to continue. Crossing the stream, I found more grass to the inch there. Frantically I searched for a spot large enough to take the tent, and eventually found a sloping site that offered possibilities. Getting the tent up, however, was quite another matter. The darkness did not help, and, although I had erected it many times before at night, the violent wind added to the nightmare. Each time I had the tent partially erected the wind flattened it, continually changing its direction to confuse matters further. For twenty frustrating minutes I battled to no avail. Pegs were being torn up as soon as I hoisted the tent into position. The inner was saturated, some of the pegs were lost in the inky blackness, and I had visions of spending the night under a boulder. I paused, then started to insert pegs and top them with boulders before erecting the inner tent. At this point the elements seemed to relent. The wind died down long enough for me to complete the task and thankfully clamber inside, absolutely exhausted from heaving large boulders around. I fully expected the whole thing to be flattened at any moment as the wind resumed its attack with a vengeance. Hurriedly I prepared a hot meal. The tent, amazingly, was still standing when the food had been devoured. Dare I get into my sleeping bag? I packed everything in case of emergency and lay in the sleeping bag watching the canvas being violently buffeted from all directions. Each hour that passed improved my position. Suddenly I became aware of the sound of running water. In the dark it assumed outrageous proportions, my imagination expecting a torrent to knock the tent over at any minute. Then I began to feel dampness inside the bag. It was not long before a small stream was running through my sleeping bag, but there was little I could do, as the whole mountainside was awash. Anyway, trying to resite the tent would have been the height of lunacy.

David Bellamy

It was a long, wet night. Sleep was virtually impossible, although I may have dozed off during the early hours. To my utter amazement the tent, though torn in places, was still standing at dawn. Bleary-eyed, I peered through the doorway. Rain was still falling, but I could at least see the valley below. There were trees down there – trees? Where was Loch Coruisk? It suddenly dawned on me that I was not on the Coruisk side, but still on the northern face, and the trees I could see were at the head of Glen Brittle.

Whilst I ate breakfast the rain stopped and the cloud rose to reveal the peaks. I then ascended my route of descent of the previous night. As I approached the top, dense mist engulfed the peak. I decided to do some scrambling on a nearby crag overlooking the adjacent corrie. The mist cleared again and once more I set off for the ridge. Halfway up, the mist returned and once more blotted everything out. This game could go on all day, I thought. I decided to climb and sit tight, and soon I was rewarded with stunning panoramic views of the main Cuillin Ridge, with Loch Coruisk nestling amidst a great horseshoe of rock. Even the wind relented for me to sketch in reasonable comfort.

LEFT:

Lock Coruisk

Seen with a topping of dark clouds, Loch Coruisk seems a dire place, hemmed in on most sides by the jagged outline of the *Cuillin. The view is looking north westwards up the loch with light bouncing off the cloud to fall over the upper reaches of the great corrie.*

However, the Cuillin always seems to have the last laugh. I abandoned this trip prematurely after a long period of dense mist, and, as I made my way down Sgurr Sgumain to Coir' a' Ghrunnda, I caught sight of some incredibly shaped rocks. One appeared like a monstrous head of some dragon, complete with spiky fang. It seemed to be laughing at me.

Rocks on Sgumain

Abhainn Strath na Sealga

14
PAINTING THE NORTHERN GIANTS

Many of the northern mountains are remote and extremely rough. Routes frequently lie across rivers impossible to cross in full spate; tracks and cairns are often non-existent; accommodation is sparse, especially in mid-winter. A high degree of self-sufficiency is therefore demanded of the mountaineer in these parts. The scale of Beinn Eighe, An Teallach, Liathach and Slioch demands a new appraisal from those used to lesser peaks. These are indeed mountains worthy of huge canvasses.

Liathach, the Grey One, a 3456-foot giant of Torridonian sandstone, lies on the north side of Glen Torridon. It impresses itself upon the traveller along the glen, soaring straight up at an alarmingly steep angle. The foreshortening of features is remarkable: what appears to be a continuous rock face from below turns out to be clusters of rock often far apart with snow in between. Never have I found a mountain so deceptive, and on my sketching there on a sunny March day I found new meaning in landscape perspective.

My first encounter with the Torridon peaks occurred one autumn when I traversed the ridge of Beinn Eighe, the Mountain of the Ice. The upper reaches were shrouded in mist. After a lunch perched on white quartzite rock high above Coire Ruadhstaca, I headed westwards, when suddenly a gap appeared in the mist to reveal a glen bathed in sunlight, thousands of feet below. In a flash it disappeared. All afternoon there were tantalizing glimpses of the landscape, while stag calls echoed across the slopes. I descended into Coire Mhic Fhearchair as the mist finally cleared, exposing the immense triple buttresses towering above the waters of the dark blue lochan. Beyond lay a vast wilderness of moors, marsh and mountains, peppered with flashes of light reflecting on pools of water caught in the late afternoon sun. I stood beside the lochan, an insignificant speck on a giant's landscape.

Further north are the smaller but equally magnetic charms of Stac Polly and Suilven. Although a mere 2009 feet high, Stac Polly is a gem, rising alone like a fairy castle amidst wild surrounding moorlands, its spires pinnacles of rock left by eroded sandstone. Some fourteen miles north of Ullapool, it presents a distinctive serrated outline as it is approached. I climbed Stac Polly one windy day when cloud hung low over the tops. There was no road winding up to the grey battlements, only a steep path over hags and heather. Continual gusts tore at the cloud, causing the mountain to appear and vanish. The fantastic shapes of weathered rocks and pinnacles were all the more enhanced when half-cloaked in swirling mists. Although sketching is at its most difficult in high winds, there were such interesting shapes that I almost forgot about the gusts. For such a small peak the feeling on top is exhilarating, with splendid views all round, despite on this occasion considerable interference from the mist. I followed my nose for subjects, scrambled up, down and across with little regard to any route. The subjects dictated my movements. Here I was in a kind of Utopia, sketching and scrambling in almost the same breath, oblivious to the wind beyond these crags.

At the north-east end of Glen Torridon lies Loch Maree, studded with wooded islands where the trees seem to grow out of the very rock. Along the shoreline stand survivors of the old Caledonian forest, providing the artist with a natural framework. The bulky mass of Slioch, the Spear, dominates the loch at its eastern end. North east of the mountain lies the Letterewe and Fisherfield wilderness, the largest wild area in Britain. Its vastness intrigued me.

One February I decided to explore the Letterewe. I spent the first night uncomfortably bivouacked beneath the stars north east of Kinlochewe, as I had not been able to find accommodation in the village. I did not have a tent with me on this occasion as I intended staying in open bothies. The next day rain was falling as I trudged past the abandoned homesteads at the Heights of Kinlochewe, and climbed towards Lochan Fada. Gradually the scenery became wilder,

Liathach Ridge

Liathach is quite unlike any other mountain in Britain, and here its peaks appear like giant pyramids, caught in the light before a storm.

Coire Mhic Fhearchair

This huge corrie stands pincered between two peaks at the western end of Beinn Eighe.

an aspect enhanced by the weather. The lochan proved to be a splendid site for lunch, the views all round providing a number of sketches as I ate, the atmosphere one of untamed desolation. Hours later I came to a tributary of the Abhainn Loch an Nid, swollen and fast-flowing. Already I'd had some horrific moments crossing streams, but this appeared much worse. In vain I searched for an easy place to cross, but there was no alternative but to wade across. The mountaineering manuals recommend that socks should be removed and boots replaced. However, it was now getting dark, and as I was already waterlogged I plunged straight in, before common sense and fear took hold of me. The ice-cold water chilled my senses and sent shocks up the body. Quickly it was over my waist. The ice-axe served as a third leg to steady my

Rocks and Pinnacles on Stac Polly

RIGHT:

Slioch and Loch Maree

OVERLEAF:

Shenavall Bothy

This bothy lies in the Strath na Sealga, at the foot of the mighty An Teallach. Beyond the bothy is Loch na Sealga.

David Bellamy

LEFT:

Lochan Fhada

Its name means long 'little loch' and it lies in the heart of the Letterewe-Fisherfield Wilderness, a truly remote spot.

RIGHT:

Beinn a' Chlaidheimh

The peak kept disappearing into a snowstorm every twenty minutes or so. In between the storms the mountain was lit up in bright sunlight: ideal sketching conditions for the watercolourist. At this time I was joined by an inquisitive ptarmigan.

faltering against the strong current that threatened to throw me off my feet. Barely halfway across, the water still deepened. The ice-axe was now of no use. There could be no retreat, for it would mean another night on the open mountain. Anyway, I could see a potential sketch ahead. Should I lose my footing I would be swept downstream, and probably pulled under by the weight of my rucksack. One final lunge and I flung myself towards the bank, gasping at the chill of icy water on my chest. Frantically I grasped at tufts of grass on the high bank, and hauled myself slowly out of the torrent, dripping like an old boot rescued from a pond.

The wetting actually invigorated me. I hastily got stuck into the sketch of Abhainn Strath na Sealga with boundless enthusiasm, although at the back of my mind I realized it was now almost impossible to reach Shenavall bothy before darkness. I finished the sketch, then found my path blocked by another stream. My euphoria evaporated at this point, but luckily the stream barely covered my knees. It was now too dark to sketch, let alone cross raging torrents. The next stream, however, made such a fearful din that I knew of its presence before I caught sight of the white foaming maelstrom. With the help of a torch that leaked water my eighth crossing was achieved without incident. By good fortune I then located the bothy and so averted an involuntary plunge into Loch na Sealga.

Dawn broke to find the landscape had been coated with a layer of snow during the night. The scenery was magnificent: down the valley Loch na Sealga lay ringed by white mountains, whilst across the glen Beinn Dearg Mor rose majestically, its triple peaks cloaked in a garb of white. It was a scene of utter peace and beauty, to which my painting did little justice.

After much sketching I climbed out of the valley and over the south-west shoulder of An Teallach, the Forge. The snow grew deeper. Angry clouds gathered and within minutes the sun had been blotted out. Soon a raging blizzard virtually halted progress, stinging my face and making route-finding a nightmare. My plan involved finding a lochan marked on the map, as this would ensure I was on the right route and the lochan itself might provide a worthwhile subject to paint. However, locating a small lochan in this white canopy would not be easy: it might even be hidden beneath the snow. The blizzard passed over and the mountains were bathed in strong sunshine again. After a short climb I spotted the deep blue water of the lochan, an oasis amidst a snowy desert. A fierce wind forced me to shelter between some rocks whilst I set about a watercolour sketch, just as another blizzard arrived to liven up proceedings. Working distant mountains into a watercolour as they are quickly disappearing behind an approaching snowstorm calls for gymnastic mixing of paints that run in all directions, as there is no time to await drying. The burnt umber had been washed off the palette by a previous downpour, so time was lost searching for the right tube of paint inside a plastic bag hidden within dark recesses of my rucksack. Inside the bag of paints my fingers found a sticky mess of red paint covering everything. The cap had loosened, causing mayhem.

I rounded the hill and came upon Loch Toll an Lochain. This must be Scotland's most spectacular corrie. I gazed in awe at the tremendous precipices falling into the lochan, its waters blue-black. Despite the numbing coldness I lingered, sketching and studying the massive corrie. Shafts of sunlight cast sparkling patches on the snowy ridge, where plumes of spindrift spun high into the air. The complicated structure of the great face took ages to render. In the shadow of the huge cliffs there was no sunshine to warm me up, only an intense cold that caused the water to freeze on the brushes, so that after the first stroke the brush was a useless blob of coloured ice. At intervals I generated heat by dancing around and clapping hands, before rushing back to continue the sketch.

Sadly, it was soon time to depart. I reluctantly left the corrie, and once below the snow-line rapidly headed north for Dundonnell. Huge horizontal slabs of rock made the going easy, and soon I descended amongst a series of waterfalls that promised many subjects for a future visit. Darkness had fallen before I found accommodation beside Little Loch Broom.

One of my most compelling targets in the northern Highlands was a close-up of the An Teallach Ridge. I approached it from the north west, across the high plateau south of Mac is Mathair, which was swept by fierce winds that carried stinging spindrift across my route. In no time my right-hand side was coated in white. After about a mile of ceaseless battering I paused in a slight depression to sketch the inhospitable scene. There was little to provide a centre of interest except small ice-covered rocks, but my aim was to capture the hostility of the conditions. It called for water-colour to indicate subtle changes of tone; pencil would not have given such a graphic impression of flying spindrift. I quickly found the brush was merely pushing coloured ice across the paper as the water froze, but even this was effective. Squinting into the eye of the storm was painful, and chunks of ice borne by the ghastly wind kept me on my toes. I put on a second pair of gloves and virtually abdicated control of the brush. Soon all four brushes were festooned with icicles, and sticking a freezing brush into your armpit to defrost it is absolute torture. I packed up, shivering, but inwardly pleased with my second sketch in the storm.

The peak I was aiming for was Bidein a' Ghlas Thuill, the Peak of the Grey Hollow, at 3483 feet the reigning summit of An Teallach. Halfway up its steep slopes, spindrift and a snowstorm engulfed me, just as a crampon slipped off my right boot, dangling uselessly from its strap. I hung on with an ice-axe whilst groping precariously for the crampon. Wind surged from behind, thrusting my cagoule up like a spinnaker, and covering everthing in spindrift. I knocked

An Teallach

Loch Toll an Lochain lies out of sight beyond a dip before the massive cliffs.

spindrift off the camera, only to find the bottom fell off it. At this point I began to question the sanity of indulging in the gentle art of watercolour painting in such a wild environment. It seemed an eternity before the crampon was secured to my boot once more. This was followed by a frantic few minutes' searching for elastic bands to hold the camera together. I then continued the upward slog, cresting the top shoulder of the peak as the storm cleared. The scene was breathtaking. Above me the summit rose from a corniced ridge, whilst huge curves of drifted snow arced down from the summit to end on rocks perched precariously over sheer cliffs. Across the void were the peaks of Glas Mheall Liath. As

I gazed dizzily down, the white snow in the corrie below was starkly cut by a thin black ribbon of a meandering burn, some 1700 feet below.

I gained the summit where the full vast panorama came into view. The eye immediately fell on the jagged outline of the main An Teallach Ridge, with the shattered face dropping down to Loch Toll an Lochain, out of sight below. Beyond the ridge were the summits of the Letterewe, whilst to the north lay Loch Broom, Stac Polly and Suilven. With frenetic haste I sketched from my vantage point, expecting another blizzard at any moment. The weather held, but it was far too late to tackle the main ridge, or even Sgurr Fiona.

Spindrift on An Teallach

I reluctantly retraced my steps down the mountain, making sure that I was off the difficult bit before it became pitch dark. Even so, it proved to be a nightmare getting back to Dundonnell in the dark.

Time now forced me to return to Kinlochewe, so I decided to recross the interior via Carmore. Cold rain stung my face as I set off from Dundonnell, a little apprehensive about my chances of crossing the larger streams. Rain squalls passed up Little Loch Broom, way beneath me as I climbed beside the roaring torrents of the Allt Airdeasaidh. I then ascended open moorland through mist and intermittent rain. Cresting a ridge below Sgurr Ruadh, I descended steep slopes towards Loch na Sealga with a growing sense of foreboding. After some time I arrived at the loch and headed for the north-west end. This would be the deciding point for the whole walk: I held no high hopes of being able to cross the outflowing river. It soon became obvious that the water level was far too high, and the current much too strong to attempt a crossing. Tantalizingly a rowing boat swung at a mooring on the opposite bank, but there was no way across. A refuge in a crack between two enormous rocks provided welcome shelter from the unceasing rain. Whilst a brew was boiling I carried out two sketches. They were both achieved by a series of jerky watercolour splotches assisted by drips falling

Summit, Bidein a' Ghlas Thuill
A quick sketch carried out as mist was clearing.

off the rocks, and embellished with a pencil. A tiny patch of red, intended to indicate bracken, quickly covered the sky area and transformed a drizzly mess into a blazing sunset. The wind gave the final *coup de grace* as it tore the sketch across my rain-soaked sleeve and confirmed it as an abstract.

An attack of the shivers made me realize it was vital to get going quickly. The choice now lay between going south east to Shenavall or north west to Gruinard, both some six miles distant. I chose the latter route, but soon found a need to regain altitude in order to cross swollen streams. The distance must have been doubled by this setback. I was lucky to emerge from the sodden wilderness before dark, thankful to have been let off relatively easily.

Some of my hardest expeditions have been in the northern Highlands. In winter, with all the extra gear and food needed, and with progress reduced to a crawl by deep

Allt Airdeasaidh Falls

To sketch this scene I was perched on dubious undergrowth over a hundred feet above the roaring waters. The gorge at this point is really spectacular, but difficult to paint from a reasonable position.

snow and swollen rivers, it is a test of endurance. There have been moments of pain when I've gashed a limb on sharp rock; moments of danger when a slip on a snow slope has threatened to send me hurtling hundreds of feet down a cliff; moments of acute discomfort during nights spent on an open mountain. All these problems have been further compounded by blizzards, storm-force winds and being wet to the skin day after day. Such moments sometimes make me wonder if it is all worth while. It is common to return from trips physically drained, with swollen feet, cuts and bruises, but it is not long before the thrill of planning the next trip is surging through my veins. For all the discomforts, hazards and trials, the sheer beauty and thrill of the mountains is unmatched and compelling. The icy crispness of the winter tops, with snow crystals sparkling in sunlight; the brooding mood of stillness before an approaching storm; or the shapes of snow-cornices sculpted by the wind: these are the memories that linger.

> What would the world be, once bereft
> Of wet and of wildness? Let them be left,
> O let them be left, wildness and wet;
> Long live the weeds and the wilderness yet.
>
> GERARD MANLEY HOPKINS

SELECTIVE BIBLIOGRAPHY

Barber, Chris, *Mysterious Wales*, Granada Publishing, 1983; Borrow, George, *Wild Wales*, Collins, 1928 (originally 1862); Crossing, William, *Crossing's Guide to Dartmoor*, originally published by *Western Morning News*, 1909, re-published by David & Charles, 1965; Hill, David, *In Turner's Footsteps*, John Murray, 1984; Murray, WH, *Mountaineering in Scotland*, Dent, 1947, republished by Diadem Books, 1979 with *Undiscovered Scotland*; Wainwright, A, *Pennine Way Companion*, Westmorland Gazette, 1968.

INDEX

ACKNOWLEDGEMENTS

I am indebted to Jean M Thomas for checking the manuscript and making sense of my dreadful scrawl, and also for allowing me to quote lines from three of her poems appearing thus:

Chapter 8: four lines on 'Castle of the winds'; Chapter 10: six lines from 'Quicksilver streams . . .'; Chapter 11: four lines on 'Fear Liath Mor'.